Wild, Wild World of Animals

Songbirds

A TIME-LIFE TELEVISION BOOK

Editor: Eleanor Graves
Series Editor: Charles Osborne
Text Editor: Richard Oulahan
    Associate Text Editor: Bonnie Johnson
    Author: Don Earnest
    Assistant Editor: Peter Ainslie
    Literary Research: Ellen Schachter
    Text Research: Maureen Duffy Benziger
    Copy Editor: Robert J. Myer
Picture Editor: Richard O. Pollard
    Picture Research: Judith Greene
    Permissions and Production: Cecilia Waters
Designer: Robert Clive
    Art Assistant: Carl Van Brunt
Production Editor: Joan Chambers

WILD, WILD WORLD OF ANIMALS
TELEVISION PROGRAM
Producers: Jonathan Donald and Lothar Wolff
This Time-Life Television Book is published by Time-Life Films, Inc.
Bruce L. Paisner, *President*
J. Nicoll Durrie, *Business Manager*

THE AUTHOR

DON EARNEST was formerly a staff writer and editor with Time-Life Books. He has contributed to two previous volumes in this series, *Insects & Spiders* and *Birds of Field & Forest,* and is the co-author of *Life in the Coral Reef.*

THE CONSULTANT

ROGER F. PASQUIER is the author of *Watching Birds: An Introduction to Ornithology.* He has worked as a curatorial assistant in the Department of Ornithology at the American Museum of Natural History in New York.

Wild, Wild World of Animals

Songbirds

Based on the television series
Wild, Wild World of Animals

Published by
TIME-LIFE FILMS

ISBN 0-913948-18-7

Library of Congress Catalog Card Number: 77-92967

Printed in the United States of America.

Contents

Introduction

by Don Earnest

"FOR, LO, THE WINTER IS PAST, the rain is over and gone; the flowers appear on the earth; the time of the singing of the birds is come. . . ." The joyous chorus of birds caroling in the early spring, which inspired Solomon to write these lines in his "Song of Songs," has long been recognized as one of nature's greatest treats—an enormous alfresco concert with thousands of participants, available to anyone willing to venture out his back door in the first light of dawn. The overwhelming majority of the songsters, and also the most melodious and vocally skilled, belong to one huge branch of the avian world whose members are scientifically known as passeriformes and more commonly as passerines but are better described by their popular name—songbirds.

Passeriformes are by far the largest order of birds—an enormous aggregation that includes more than 5,000 of the approximately 9,000 living species and contains about three fifths of the estimated 100 billion feathered creatures on the globe. Among the order are many of the most familiar birds—robins, thrushes, finches, larks, mockingbirds, buntings, warblers, swallows, sparrows, jays, crows, ravens. It also includes an unusually large complement of some of the most exotic creatures on earth—the peacocklike lyrebirds of Australia, the brilliant sunbirds of Africa and Asia, the nectar-sipping akiapolaau of Hawaii and the birds of paradise, which awed the Europeans who first saw their luxuriant plumage.

Most passerines are small to medium-sized birds, ranging from five to 10 inches in length. But some common songbirds like wrens and titmice are often under four inches and a few of the tiniest tropical species measure no more than three. At the other extreme the raven is a good two feet long and the lyrebird is over three feet from the tip of its bill to the end of its trainlike tail.

All are land birds, and they are at home in every continent except the frozen wastelands of Antarctica. They have adapted better than any other order of birds to almost every conceivable environment. The alpine chough (pronounced "chuff"), a distant relative of the crow, is an inhabitant of mountain peaks and has been encountered by climbers on the Himalayan slopes of Mount Everest at elevations approaching 20,000 feet. The desert lark survives on the parched sands of the Sahara, where the temperature soars to over 150° F., by catching insects and drinking dew among rocks and scant vegetation. The snow bunting builds its nest in the cold light of the brief Arctic summer 400 miles from the North Pole and in winter does not retreat much farther south than northern Europe and America. The black-capped chickadee often rides out the winter in the middle of Alaska where the thermometer plunges to 50° F. below zero. One family of passerines, aptly named dippers, has even taken to water. Staking a claim to a stretch of a rushing mountain stream, a dipper passes most of its day diving for food, swimming under water

Sparrows and chrysanthemums decorate a Japanese lacquer box.

with its wings and nesting more often than not behind the curtain of a waterfall. Quite a few songbirds, such as meadowlarks and blackbirds in North America and the sparrowlike weaverbirds of Africa and Asia, have adapted to fields, plains, steppes, savannas and other grasslands. Others, such as starlings, are able to live in almost any environment, and the ubiquitous house sparrows thrive in the canyons of Manhattan. The names of the cliff swallow, barn swallow, seaside sparrow and swamp sparrow give a precise indication of their special haunts.

Most passerines, however, are arboreal, making their homes in trees ranging from scrub oak thickets to dense tropical rain forests. In a typical temperate woodland, they divide up the habitat for perching, foraging and often nesting. Some claim the upper canopy. Others take the middle and lower levels of foliage, and still others claim the trunks, the underbrush and the forest floor. These birds are superbly designed by nature for a life among the trees. Also known as perching birds, passerines are notable for their feet. Each foot has three toes pointing forward and one backward. The hind toe is exceptionally strong, and when it closes around a branch to join the middle toe, the bird commands an unyielding grip almost like the jaws of a vise. As uniquely adapted in their own way to an arboreal environment as a duck's webbed feet are to water, the songbird's feet operate without any conscious effort on the part of the bird, automatically clamping and locking together the instant they come into contact with a branch or twig, and they maintain their tight pincer-like grip even while the bird sleeps. For songbirds that have moved out of the trees, the toes function equally well for perching on reeds, fence wires and even grass stems.

Passerines also have some distinctive behavioral characteristics that are shared with very few other birds. All songbirds are born unseeing, naked and so totally helpless that they must be nurtured and cared for until they are able to fend for themselves. As a result, songbirds have evolved an elaborate system of instinctive parental behavior that ranges from nest building to teaching their fledglings how to hunt for food. In addition, the colorful, gaping mouths of begging songbird nestlings are rare outside the passerine order.

Babies that are as defenseless as young songbirds are usually found only among the most highly evolved animals. And this characteristic, along with the intelligence and skill shown by many passerines, notably crows, indicates that they are almost certainly the most recently developed order of birds. They started to take their own separate evolutionary path about 60 million years ago—only yesterday when compared to such birds as the waterfowl, which date back nearly twice as far. And these highly adaptable creatures are still continuing to evolve, flexibly adjusting themselves to changing food supplies

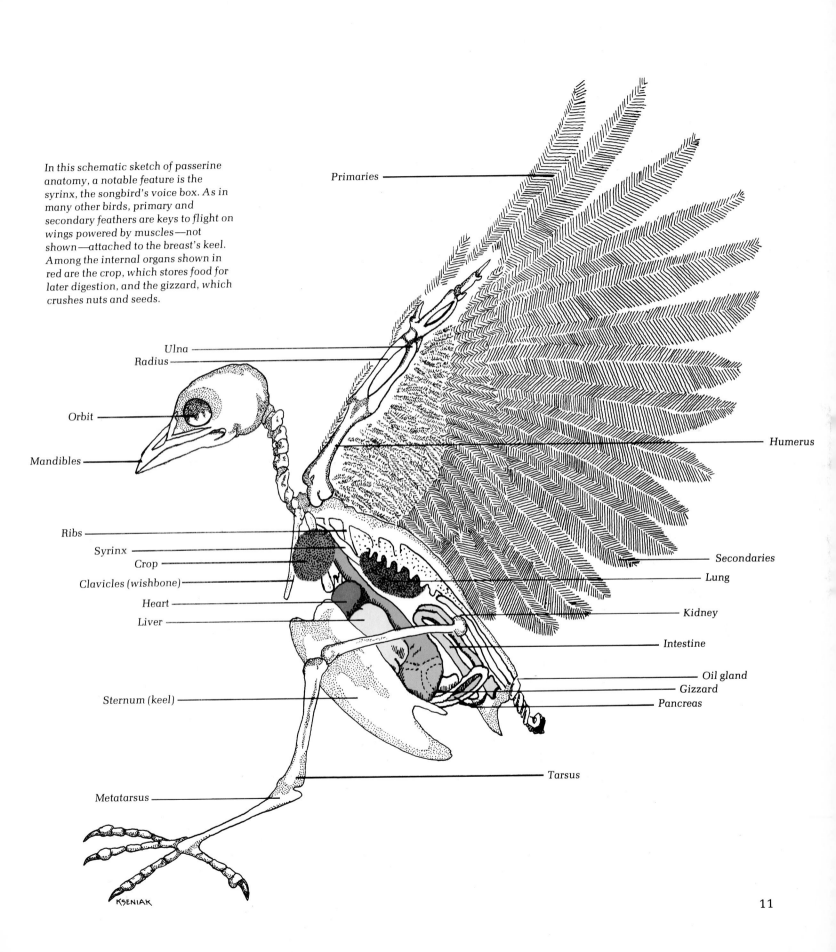

In this schematic sketch of passerine anatomy, a notable feature is the syrinx, the songbird's voice box. As in many other birds, primary and secondary feathers are keys to flight on wings powered by muscles—not shown—attached to the breast's keel. Among the internal organs shown in red are the crop, which stores food for later digestion, and the gizzard, which crushes nuts and seeds.

Primaries

Ulna
Radius

Orbit

Mandibles

Humerus

Ribs
Syrinx
Crop
Clavicles (wishbone)
Heart
Liver

Secondaries
Lung

Kidney

Intestine

Oil gland
Gizzard
Pancreas

Sternum (keel)

Tarsus

Metatarsus

KSENIAK

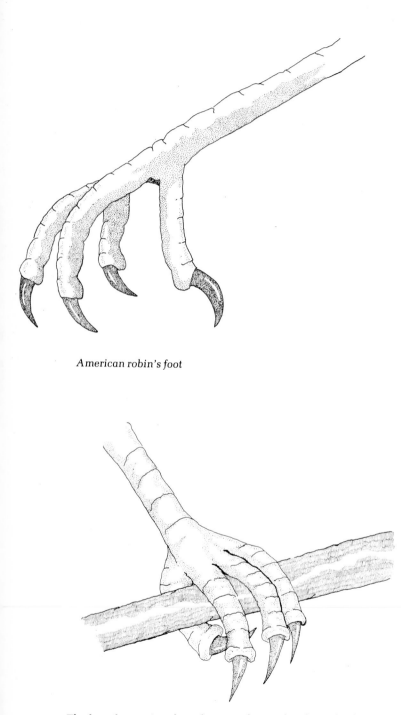

American robin's foot

The feet of passerines have four toes that work independently and flexibly, with a hind toe (top) that is opposable, worked by a system of muscles and tendons that reflexively closes into a fist in perching, permitting the bird to sleep without falling.

and living accommodations in today's world—something that no other group of birds does so well.

One unusual group of passerines has the distinction of providing at least a part of the inspiration for Charles Darwin's theory of evolution. They present in miniature a good example of how at least one type of evolution works. On his famous voyage around the world, the great naturalist stopped in September 1835 to examine the flora and fauna of the Galápagos Islands in the Pacific, several hundred miles off the coast of Ecuador. There he discovered 13 species of songbirds, now known as Darwin's finches, which were remarkably alike in plumage and physique, and in fact seemed to have only one notable difference: the shape and size of their beaks. The conclusion was inescapable: The birds must be descended from a common ancestor, probably from South American finches that were blown out to the islands by a storm. Finding the available food supply limited, the birds evolved new forms to exploit different niches in the insular environment. Their plumage had changed little with time, but each species had developed a beak to match its diet and they ranged from heavy, blunt bills suitable for crushing seeds to longer, lightweight ones for picking insects out of foliage. Two species had even assumed the role of a woodpecker, but not having a tongue long enough to reach the grubs and other insects hidden in holes in trees and plants they ingeniously learned how to use a cactus spine to pry them out.

In addition to these assets, most passerines are skilled aviators, and several make a round-trip journey of a few thousand miles each year during their spring and fall migrations. As in most birds, every part of their body functions to facilitate the conquest of air. Not only are their bones light and hollow, but to lessen air resistance their bodies are streamlined, and all heavy muscles and major organs are concentrated in the trunk near the center of gravity. Wings are the minimum number of feathers arranged on a light-

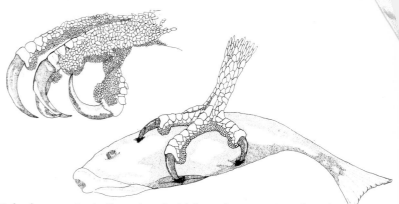

weight frame of hollow bones connected by tendons to the body muscles. The whole system is an aerodynamic wonder that is shaped to provide lift in a current of air. To meet the enormous energy demands of flying, heart and lungs and air sacs in and around the bones work together with the circulatory system to provide oxygen and nourishment quickly and efficiently. Essential to its adept flight is the passerine's extremely well-developed eyesight—capable of adjusting rapidly when the bird goes from direct sunlight to darkness in dense foliage or of making sudden switches of focus as the bird scans the sky for predators and then instantly pinpoints a tiny insect an inch away. With all this marvelous equipment, songbirds achieve a flight speed that is impressive for their small size—an average of 20 miles per hour, produced by a relatively rapid five flaps of the wings per second. Some, such as swallows and starlings, slide between a series of fast flaps, and a few, such as some warblers and the ruby-crowned kinglet, can hover briefly in one spot like a hummingbird.

Birds of prey are typically equipped with long, sharp, curving talons that are designed for clutching. When the claws of an osprey (above) fasten on a fish they automatically dig in, and the undersurfaces of the toes are rough, giving the raptor a firmer grip on slippery quarry.

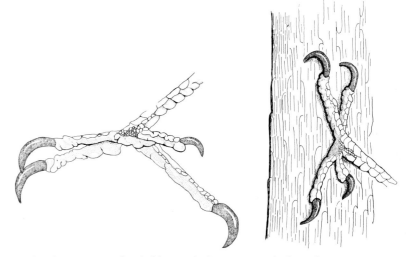

Passerines truly excel in the variety and complexity of the sounds that they make. It may be claimed that they are the best vocalists, not only among birds but in the entire animal kingdom, although man, who infuses his music with his culture and civilization, is a special case. Technically, songbirds outshine man in the range and rapidity of their delivery. It is not surprising that many songbirds take their names from their vocal skill. Warblers and babblers are the descriptive names for large groups of passerines. And of course there is a song sparrow, a song thrush, a singing starling and a singing honey eater as well as a musician wren. On his first encounter with the elaborate orchestration of the latter, Henry Bates, a 19th-century explorer of the Amazon, observed: "When its unique tones first strike a listener's ear, he can only suspect a human voice as their cause. Some musical fellow must be searching for fruit in the thickets and be singing a few tones to cheer himself up. Then the

Woodpeckers' toes are divided fore and aft in pairs, with claws that are hooked, enabling the birds to cling to the surface of a tree trunk (above) while they drill holes, or move about freely in their vertical world, searching for insects under the bark.

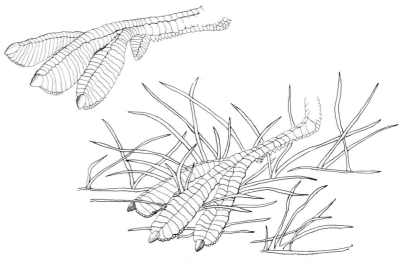

The palmate foot of a grebe is not webbed like the toes of a duck or other water birds. But it is just as well adapted to swimming, with the toes flattening out like paddles when the bird is thrusting forward in the water, and folding back to minimize friction on the return stroke.

sounds become softer and more plaintive; they sound as if produced by a small flute and although it makes no sense, one is still convinced for a moment that someone must be playing an instrument."

Many songbirds have acquired their names as people have endeavored to describe their songs and other calls: chiffchaff, chickadee, phoebe, towhee, pewee, dickcissel. In Mexico, a songbird that frequently and loudly broadcasts a tuneful *ho-say-ma-re-ah* is widely known as José-Maria. Some others have earned their distinctive titles by a vocal characteristic. The grasshopper sparrow makes a dry rasping trill like its namesake. The gray catbird reacts to a challenge with a long whining *mew*. The nightingale is often a midnight soloist. The whistling thrushes echo their melodic whistles off the slopes of the Himalayas. The laughing thrushes fill the shadowy teak forests of Burma with peals of sinister laughter so ghostly that one observer thought they would be better described as feathered goblins.

Most of the vocal productions of songbirds are calls—short, abrupt signals. The song sparrow, for example, has at least 24 such calls. These sounds keep migrating flocks together, tell of the discovery of food, help mates find each other in tall grass or dense foliage and advise parents that their nestlings are hungry or their fledglings are lost. Many also warn of danger, and among some birds, different calls may tell them whether the threat comes from a bird of prey above or a predator on the ground, while yet another may signal "all clear." Such alarms are often understood by different songbird species in a single locality so that all the species benefit from the warnings of one.

While their calls are more numerous and varied than those of other birds, passerines reach unique heights in the intricate music of their songs—in the pitch, tone, duration and complexity of notes and in the richness and beauty of their melodies. Most listeners agree that the finest singers are the thrushes—a family that includes not only the song thrush but also the nightingale and the American robin. But many wrens are accomplished musicians, and so are some sparrows. The performance of any of these gifted vocalists is enough to make a human musician wince with envy. There are sometimes several hundred separate sounds in the song, and they are grouped into motifs and strung in phrases. Altogether, the performance takes less than a minute. The song sparrow emits 15 to 17 notes per second, each note precisely modulated in pitch and amplitude and each distinctly separate. Comparison between this vocal ability and that possessed by humans is impossible. To match the song sparrow an operatic soprano would have to deliver a flawless recital of an aria at a hundred times the normal tempo. Moreover, the song sparrow may repeat its aria 200 times an hour. The performance record seems to be held by the indefatigable red-eyed vireo, which sings as often as 22,000 times a day.

Singing with this frequency occurs only at the beginning of the breeding season, usually in spring, and most often the singer is a male claiming a mating territory. At that time of year the songs also reach their maximum in intensity and melodiousness. And since most passerines are in peak singing form at daybreak, it is during these months and at that hour that the full chorus is heard. Starting about an hour before sunrise, each bird adds its voice to the growing symphony of sounds, seemingly on cue, as if following a score that requires the wren, for example, to chime in exactly 21.55 minutes before the sun breeches the horizon. Although the male nearly always has the leading role, sometimes his mate joins him in a duet. Among a few wrens this "part-singing" becomes an antiphonal exchange so closely synchronized that it is impossible for the listener to tell which bird is vocalizing unless he happens to be between them. In addition to these sunrise arias, songbirds utter more subdued tunes, such as the softly whispered melodies couples' exchange during courtship or the low melody that a mother sometimes uses to entice her newborns to eat. Sometimes birds sing at any hour, seemingly for nothing more than pure joy on a bright sunny day. And there are many instances of the parents hailing the departure of their young from the nest with a spontaneous outburst of song.

A few passerines carry their vocal facility to an extreme by imitating the songs of other birds. The marsh warbler has a repertoire of nearly 40 stolen tunes in addition to its own, and jays and European redstarts are also talented song pirates. Other mimics do not limit themselves to birdsongs. A crested lark once re-created a shepherd's whistles so well that his dog responded to four different commands issued by the bird rather than the master. The lyrebird of Australia reproduces the hooting of owls and the "laughing jackass" cackling of kookaburras along with noises such as automobile horns. The mockingbird repeats frogs' croaks, dogs' barks and crickets' chirps as well as screeching wheels and squeaking hinges. One of these master mimics reportedly piped up during an outdoor performance of Prokofiev's *Peter and the Wolf* in Washington, D.C., and started imitating a flute that was imitating birdcalls.

Even though the versatility of such clever imitations is impressive, it is still the carefully controlled lyric cadences of a gifted singer that brings the greatest joy to the listener, especially when it strikes the ear unexpectedly in the solitude of the wilderness. On a trip to New York's Mohawk River Valley in the 1830s, John James Audubon, the great artist and naturalist, reported hearing the sweet song of the rose-breasted grosbeak: "The evening was calm and beautiful, and the sky sparkled with stars. . . . suddenly there burst on my soul the serenade of the rose-breasted bird—so rich, so mellow, so loud in the stillness of the night, that sleep fled. Never did I enjoy music more. . . ."

15

Songbird Families

The birds of the passerine world are wondrously varied, ranging in size and plumage from tiny, tawny wrens to large, ornately feathered birds of paradise. But since all songbirds belong to the most recently evolved order of birds, they share many physical as well as behavioral characteristics. On a summer stroll through nearly any woods, the casual observer cannot help being struck by the apparent similarities in many of these small creatures. In some instances even experts must make a careful examination to distinguish between passerine birds that may be only distantly related. On the other hand, a few closely related birds—such as blue jays, with their jaunty azure backs and white breasts, and crows, with their drab parson's garb—are surprisingly different in both appearance and size. Against this complex background, one of the greatest triumphs of ornithology has been identifying and naming all the members of this largest avian order.

Passerine common names are another matter: European explorers and settlers have given the birds they encountered the names of familiar—and often similar looking—birds from home. Thus, a so-called redstart or blackbird or robin in Asia or the Americas may be a totally different species from its European namesake.

Attempts at classification started early. In the seventh century B.C. the Assyrians tried grouping birds by habitat. During their golden age the Greeks also established loose categories, and Aristotle, who was a naturalist as well as a philosopher, identified over 170 varieties. In the first century A.D. the Roman scholar Pliny the Elder took a great step forward by distinguishing among birds according to the structure of their feet.

It was not until the middle of the 18th century, however, that Linnaeus, one of the fathers of modern biology, provided a comprehensive system for categorizing birds and all other living creatures. Linnaeus' system is the familiar hierarchy of kingdom, phylum, class, order, family, genus and species—sometimes with the prefix sub- added to refine the groupings further. Working with this system, scientists soon recognized that passerines, with their many common characteristics, formed a distinct order within the class of feathered creatures known as birds.

Although ornithologists still disagree on the exact number, the more than 5,000 species of passerines discovered so far have been divided into 69 families. Some of these families consist of only one unusual species in an isolated locale, such as the palm chat, which builds communal nests atop palm trees in the West Indies. Other families are enormous and widespread, found in every habitable part of the globe. An example is the finch family, which includes cardinals, grosbeaks, buntings, towhees, juncos and sparrows, as well as finches—a total of nearly 375 species. Superficial similarities frequently provide the first clue to bird relationships, but sometimes they can be misleading. The meadowlark in North America and the yellow-throated longclaw of Africa, which both have dappled brown back plumage and yellow breasts marked with black horseshoes, could easily be taken for twins. Yet they belong to widely separated families that happened upon the same successful formula for surviving in similar grassland habitats. But this can be confirmed only because scientists back up their initial hunches through careful analysis of more fundamental links, such as the arrangement of feathers on the wings and scales on the legs.

In field studies of bird behavior ornithologists have learned to distinguish quickly among the few hundred different species of birds, mostly passerines, that live in or pass through a region. The methods they use are very similar to those employed by the growing number of amateurs who have turned bird watching into one of the most popular outdoor pastimes, with over a million people in the United States as active participants. Size, shape, coloration and markings in themselves are often dead giveaways—especially when coupled with location and time of year. The four species of tanager that occur in North America—the scarlet, hepatic, summer and western—have different breeding ranges and physical characteristics, and such early fall migrants as swallows are not likely to be spotted in the north after September.

But sometimes birders must look for other clues. Airborne meadowlarks and starlings, for example, have almost identical silhouettes, but meadowlarks have a distinctive way of flying—several fast flaps followed by a long soaring sail that is quite unlike the starlings' more regular manner of flight. Similarly, the way sparrows hop, wrens cock their tails and swifts catch insects on the wing are aids in identification. And, of course, since passerines are songbirds, they can often be recognized by their distinctive songs and calls—so much so that many experienced birders do not even have to raise their binoculars to identify birds, just so long as they can hear the song.

A western meadowlark on a Colorado plain

Its azure plumes and fine crest make the blue jay easy to identify. Known to attack nestlings of other songbirds, jays fiercely defend their own young until they are able to fend for themselves.

Head of the Class

Among the 69 families of passerine birds (17 of the most familiar and intriguing are pictured on the following pages) and indeed among all birds, one of the most advanced groups on the avian evolutionary tree is the family Corvidae. The 100 species that make up the family include, among others, the ravens, crows, jays and magpies seen on these pages, intelligent birds that have adapted well to the presence of man. Corvids are hardy creatures that can withstand extremes of temperature and tend not to migrate. They are distinguished by sharp, strong bills that are used variously to hammer, tear, crack, probe and crush, enabling the birds to eat just about anything. Their diet includes everything from seeds to berries to small mammals and young birds and even carrion.

Like all corvids, the green magpies of Asia show no sexual differentiation in their colors. Both male and female have the same striking plumage.

The vivid blues, greens and yellows of the green jay's feathers (above) act as an effective camouflage in the dappled sunlight and shade of the forest.

Although large for a songbird, the pied crow (left), at 18 inches, is one of the smaller corvids. Common to sub-Saharan Africa, pied crows often feast on urban garbage dumps.

The raven (above) is supported on strong legs and large feet, effective perching and grasping limbs possessed by all corvids. Twenty-seven inches long, it is the largest corvid.

Shining Robes

The cedar waxwing (left) and its close relative, the species of silky flycatcher called phainopepla (below), are slender birds with prominent crests and soft velvety plumage. The waxwings are named for the waxy appearance of the tips of the secondary wing feathers on many adults, both male and female. (These shiny wingtips may have a function in courtship display.) The phainopepla's name is derived from the Greek and means "shining robe," an apt description of the male bird's silky black plumage.

Both birds are sociable and travel in flocks, sometimes in large numbers. They wander like nomads in search of fruit and berries; nesting relatively late in the season, they postpone mating until the fruit in their breeding grounds has begun to ripen.

A cedar waxwing (left) shows off its black face mask, yellow tail band and waxy feather markings. Like all waxwings, the cedars are highly gregarious, forming tight-knit groups that stay together through the year.

A male phainopepla (above) pauses to rest during one of his long, wandering flights. Of the four species of silky flycatchers, the phainopepla is the only one to breed in the United States, nesting in the arid Southwest.

The wood thrush (left) retains as an adult the characteristic splotches on its breast that mark all members of the thrush family when they are young. The eastern bluebird (above) is widely known as one of the first harbingers of spring, though bluebirds often do not migrate at all but remain in the northern limits of their eastern American habitat throughout the worst of winter. The robin, with its cheerful chirp, sweet song and brick-red breast is perhaps the most notable herald of spring. The western robin at right is one of seven slightly differing subspecies of the familiar bird.

Spring's Harbingers

Members of the family Turdidae, the thrushes include some of the best known and loved of all birds—robins, bluebirds, veeries, nightingales—and inhabit every region of the world except parts of the Arctic and some Pacific islands. Yet ornithologists are hard pressed to define just what thrushes are, and many authorities group them together in an enormous superfamily with the closely related Old World warblers and flycatchers, and babblers and chats.

One characteristic of all thrushes, though, is the speckled or spotted underbelly that they all have as nestlings—an identification that many members of the family lose when they shed their juvenile plumage and gain their first adult feathers. What remains as a way to spot a thrush is music—for the thrushes include some of the most operatic of all birds. Whether the European nightingale or the hermit or wood thrush of North America is the greatest songster of the bird kingdom is debatable, but one thing is certain: The very name "thrush" is now a dictionary definition of an extraordinary singer.

The Eurasian robin above is a small, plump, friendly bird that is especially associated with English gardens and hedgerows, and is the celebrated Cock Robin or Robin Redbreast of legend and story.

23

The Mimics

The largest musical repertoires among the passerines belong to the Mimidae, a family of 31 species found only in the Americas that includes the mockingbirds, the gray catbirds and the thrashers. While the Mimidae as a family are generally known for their excellent voices and remarkable facility for mimicry, some species have poor voices and only limited ability at imitating the sounds of other creatures. The curve-billed thrasher (below), for example, emits a clear melodious whistle but is hardly a distinguished vocalist, considerably inferior to the mockingbird, the undisputed star of the family. One mockingbird at Boston's Arnold Arboretum performed 87 different tunes within a seven-minute period, repeating each tune several times. Another was able to imitate 39 birdsongs and 50 birdcalls—as well as the very unbirdlike sounds of a frog and a cricket. Mockingbirds also have distinctive songs of their own that make up much of their repertoire.

The vocal abilities of the gray catbirds vary greatly from one individual to another. While some are, at best, mediocre songsters, others compete admirably with the mockingbirds in the variety of their musical phrases and the pace at which they sing them.

The monotones of the mockingbird's gray-and-white plumage (above) contrast with its colorful song. Mockingbirds can be heard all year long and are among the few nocturnal singers.

A curve-billed thrasher (left) pauses on a branch, showing off the sharply curved beak that it uses to toss aside dead leaves and probe for insects.

A slender gray catbird (left) stands alert, ready to sound out the feline meow it utters when it is alarmed or when it is defending its territory against intruders.

Fussbudgets

Their family name, Troglodytidae, suggests that wrens are troglodytes, or cave dwellers. But the description is imprecise. While most wrens do seek some sort of hollow or cavelike enclosure to nest in, many do not. The mountain wren builds a conventional cup nest, and the cactus wren (below) often beds down in the thorny bosom of a cholla cactus. Other wrens nest in astonishing places—a sock, a tin can, the engine of an abandoned automobile. And, perhaps more than any other bird, the house wren (right) has taken to the snug security of man-made birdhouses.

The second dictionary definition of troglodyte, "unso-cial, brutish, seclusive," is even less applicable to wrens. Cheeky and bold little creatures they undoubtedly are, ready to take on birds twice their size in a dispute over a nest, and a female wren is the noisiest nag in the bird kingdom when she feels her mate is being laggard in his nest-building duties. But the syncopated duets of a mated pair are among the most beautiful birdsongs. And the tiny birds usually roost together companionably. In the moors of northern Scotland and the Shetland Islands dozens of winter wrens—the only Old World species—will huddle together to escape the wuthering cold of a January night.

The cactus wren above is nonchalantly at home among the thorns of a prickly pear. Birds of the southwestern United States and Mexico, they consume prodigious numbers of insects.

Snug in its tree-hole nest, a house wren surveys the world (right). Most wrens use their nests not only to hatch as many as 16 young each summer but as year-round shelters for the adults.

Birds of the Colorado Valley

by Elliott Coues

Elliott Coues was one of the most respected American ornithologists of the 19th century, a co-founder of the American Ornithologists' Union. Born in 1842, he served in the army from 1862 to 1881 and traveled widely throughout the United States, studying birds in his spare time. Both Birds of the Northwest *and* Birds of the Colorado Valley *were written during his army service. Coues' greatest work, the authoritative* The Key to North American Birds, *was published posthumously in 1903. Coues combined a scientific background with the keen observation of a skilled reporter, as demonstrated below in his description of the nesting habits of house wrens from* Birds of the Colorado Valley.

Their notion seems to be, that whatever place they select, be it large or small, must be completely filled with a lot of rubbish before they can feel comfortable about it. When they nest in a knot-hole, or any cavity of inconsiderable dimensions, the structure is a mass of sticks and other trash of reasonable bulk; but the case is otherwise when they get behind a loose weather-board, for instance, where there is room enough for a dozen nests; then they never know when to stop. I witnessed a curious illustration of their "insane" propensities in one case where a pair found their way through a knot-hole into one of those small sheds which stands in the back-yard, with a well-worn path leading to the house, showing its daily use. (It should be premised that a wren likes to get into its retreat through the smallest possible orifice; if the entrance be small enough, there cannot be too much room inside; and, when the hole is unnecessarily large, it is often closed up to the right size.) Having entered through a nice little hole, into a dark place, the birds evidently supposed it was all right inside, and began to build in a corner under the roof, where the joists came together. Though annoyed by frequent interruption, the indefatigable little creatures, with almost painful diligence, lugged in their sticks till they had made a pile that would fill a bushel, and I cannot say they would not have filled the whole shed had they not been compelled to desist; for they were voted a nuisance, and the hole was stopped up. The size of the sticks they carried in was enormous in comparison with their own stature; it seemed as if they could not lift them, much less drag the crooked pieces through such a narrow orifice. These coarse materials, it will be remembered, are only the foundation of a nest, as it were; their use in places where there is no real occasion for such a mass of trash is evidently the remaining trace of primitive habits. Inside this pile of material, there is a compact cup-like nest proper, of various fine soft vegetable and animal substances. The birds are extremely prolific, ordinarily laying six or eight eggs; and they will continue to deposit more if the nest be robbed—sometimes to the number of three or four full clutches. The eggs themselves are too well known to require description. As to the sites of the nest, it is almost impossible to speak in specific terms. The old hat Audubon drew has become historic; the sleeve or pocket of a coat hung up in an outhouse—a box in a chaise from which the birds were often ejected, and to which they as often returned—boxes, jars, or gourds set up for Martins—skull of an ox or horse—nest of another bird—are among the odd places the birds have been known to fancy. In the West, favorite locations for Parkman's Wren are a rift in an old stump or log, or the crevice between a strip of partially detached bark and the trunk of a tree—places which give full scope for its inveterate liking to fill up a cavity to an unlimited extent and then barricade the entrance.

Friendly and Fearless

Many songbirds have adjusted smoothly to the presence of man, but perhaps the most adaptable of all is the family Paridae, which includes the tits and titmice and the chickadees. Friendly, curious, often noisy creatures, they are commonly seen flitting from one branch to another in search of the insects and larvae they feed on, seemingly oblivious to the presence of humans. Most of the Paridae are small birds less than six inches long. The sexes look alike, mostly gray and brown in color.

Tits and chickadees are generally cavity dwellers, nesting in naturally formed openings in trees or in abandoned woodpecker holes. Some species excavate their own holes in the soft wood of rotting tree stumps. Apart from its normal function as a nursery, the nest also serves as a shelter for adult birds from the winter cold and a refuge from predators such as hawks, jays and owls all year long.

The black-capped chickadee is a year-round resident of Canada and the northern United States, surviving the winters on a diet of dormant forest insect life.

A tufted titmouse clings to the trunk of a tree (left) as it plucks insects from cracks in the bark. A familiar resident of eastern North America, this six-inch bird also feasts on acorns and seeds.

At just over four inches in length, the blue tit is one of the smallest and most vulnerable among the Paridae family, which suffers an unusually high annual mortality rate of 75 percent. To compensate, some species raise two broods a year. Others, like the blue tit, lay large clutches timed to hatch with the spring appearance of green caterpillars to feed the young.

A Garbling of Warblers

The taxonomists have saddled the warblers of the Western Hemisphere with a misnomer. For most, their warbling is hardly worthy of the name. They tend to be poor if persistent singers with weak voices, though one exception, the yellow-breasted chat, has a flutelike song that it often sings in the middle of the night. These North American birds have been called wood warblers in an effort to distinguish them from Old World warblers, a large and completely unrelated passerine family which includes some superb singers that are also usually woodland birds.

Though the name "warbler" may be misleading, the designations of many of the individual species of wood warblers are clues to either their appearance or likely location. The palm warbler is found in Florida palm trees in winter; the Cape May and Nashville warblers are seen in those areas during migration. The hooded warbler and the black-throated gray warbler shown here are accurate reflections of their names, as is the prothonotary warbler, named for its orange and yellow plumage, which is similar to robes worn by prothonotaries, or papal secretaries.

A single bright yellow spot in front of each eye touches up the muted plumage of the black-throated gray warbler (opposite), a native of the mountains of the American West.

The hooded warbler (above) is a wide-ranging North American warbler. The bold head markings—typical of many warblers—probably play a role in courtship display.

Contrary Clan

The family name Icteridae derives from the Greek word for jaundice, or "yellow"; by that definition all icterids should be yellow birds. But while yellow or orange plumage is common enough among them, it is by no means universal, as the gallery on these pages demonstrates. Icterid behavior, habits and habitats are also extremely variable. Icterids are, in fact, among the most adaptable of all birds. Most are nonmigratory, tropical natives, but many, like the bobolink, are remarkable long-distance travelers. Meadowlarks build globular nests of grass on the ground, oropendolas weave intricate six-foot-long stockings in the topmost boughs of the rain forest, and cowbirds deposit their eggs in the nests of other birds. Some are loners; others flock together by the millions. About the only common denominator among icterids is that all are New World birds.

A tropical oriole, the troupial (above), is a popular cage bird in its native South America, valued for its handsome plumage and for its ability as a mimic of birds and humans.

Marshlands of South America are the habitat of the scarlet-headed blackbird (above), which, except for the color of its head, closely resembles its North American distant cousin at right.

The musical bobolink (above) migrates annually from southern Canada to central South America. In the United States South it was once regarded both as a pest for its raids on rice fields and as a table delicacy for its savory flesh.

Resting on a clump of flowering gorse in the Falkland Islands, a long-tailed meadowlark (left) with its crimson breast looks quite unlike its familiar white, brown and yellow namesake of North America.

A yellow-headed blackbird (above), a gregarious marshland denizen of the United States West from the prairies to the Pacific, often shares the same territory—but never interbreeds—with the colorful red-winged blackbird.

A Tropical Spectrum

The warmer parts of the New World, especially the humid lowland forests of Central and South America, are home to most of the approximately 220 species of tanagers. Among these four- to eight-inch birds, a majority are relatively weak songsters, but their resplendent, multi-hued plumage more than compensates for their colorless vocalizations. Their feathers are often a patchwork of lavish shades ranging in color from deep purple to turquoise blue, saffron yellow to emerald green—the classic hues of tropical birds.

Tanagers are distinguished by short, strong conical bills and the well-developed feet and legs characteristic of birds that spend most of their time in the trees. They feed on seeds and berries as well as on insects that they either pluck from the undersides of leaves or from under the bark of trees. Tanagers inhabit the jungle canopy where the dappled shadows created by the play of sunlight on leaves obscure even their dazzling colors from the eyes of such predators as hawks.

Paradise tanager (above)

Scarlet tanager (below)

Blue-necked tanager

Golden tanager

Multicolored tanager

Western tanager

37

Finch Fraternity

The finch family is a large and diverse bird grouping that ranges throughout the world except in Australia and some oceanic islands. Because finches are primarily seed eaters, and because seeds are a fairly recent evolutionary development in plants, American ornithologists theorize that finches must be among the most recently evolved of birds. The theory helps explain the large number of species (some 375) in the finch family: Because there was little competition for the environmental niche opened by this new food source, the finches evolved rapidly and proliferated.

Four members of the finch family are pictured on these pages. The rufous-sided towhee (below), ranges from British Columbia to Maine and south to Guatemala. The chaffinch (below, right) ranges across northern Europe and is expanding eastward each year. At right is the American cardinal, once primarily a southern bird but now found as far north as southern Ontario. The red crossbill (opposite) lives in coniferous forests of the Northern Hemisphere.

A male rufous-sided towhee fans his tail in a courtship display (above). A white spot near the tail, not normally visible, shows in a flash when the bird takes off, alerting others to danger or momentarily distracting a predator.

Red feathers aglow, a male cardinal perches in a Florida thicket (above). So strong is the male's instinct to feed young birds that cardinals often feed the young of other species.

A chaffinch (left) perches on a twig. When Linnaeus, the Swedish systematist, noticed only male chaffinches wintering in Sweden, he named the birds coelebs, or "without marriage." Later he learned that female chaffinches migrate farther away from home than males.

Equipped with a scissorlike bill that is adept at snipping pine-cone scales open, a red crossbill (right) sits on a stump in Oregon. Crossbills migrate into the Deep South when pine cones are scarce in Canada, northern New England and southeast Alaska.

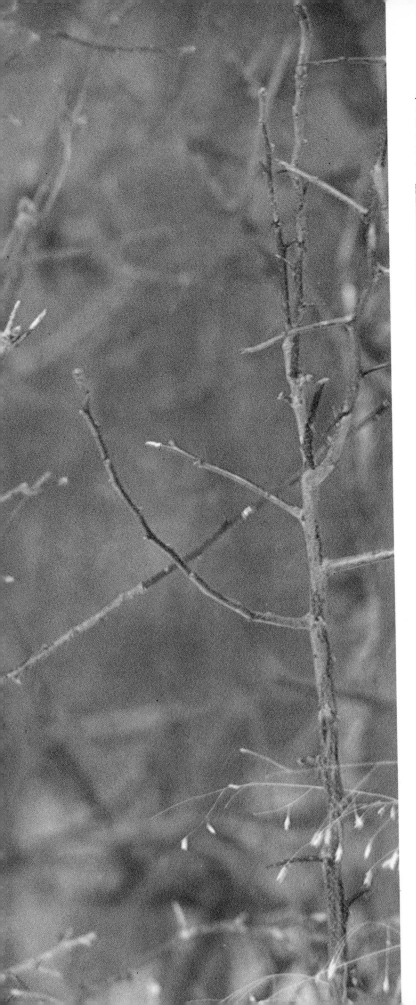

An evening grosbeak alights on a dogwood tree in British Columbia (below). Once identified as a western-dwelling nocturnal bird, it is now known to be neither. Its range has expanded east to Massachusetts.

Three Harris' sparrows blend into woodland twigs (left). Considered by some to be the handsomest of the sparrows, Harris' sparrows breed in northwestern Canada, wintering as far south as Texas.

The vermilion flycatcher (above), the most vividly colored member of its family, has the Latin name "fire-head" —Pyrocephalus rubinus. Flycatchers employ a wide range of styles and materials for their nests; vermilions build a flat cup decorated with lichen.

The brisk, jaunty ash-throated flycatcher (left) is an extremely adaptable bird. It ranges from north to south in the American West and is at home both in below-sea-level deserts and in mountain forests.

The banded Peruvian cock-of-the-rock (right) is a ground-level bird that prowls the forest floor in the eastern Andean slopes from Colombia to Peru.

Amiable Tyrants, Flashy Mountaineers

The birds on these pages are among the handsomest members of two passerine families: the tyrant flycatchers and the cotingas. They are grouped together within a large superfamily, the suboscines, or primitive songbirds. The flycatchers, which, despite their name, are not all tyrannical, have their family's typical wreaths of tiny bristles around their bills. The vermilion flycatcher (opposite, above), with its brilliant plumage, ranges from the southwestern United States to Argentina to the Galápagos Islands. The ash-throated flycatcher (opposite, below) has a novel and effective way of frightening off predators: a piece of snakeskin prominently displayed in its nest, or a bit of shiny plastic or cellophane.

The exotic bird below, with its flame-colored feathers and rakish cocked-hat crest, is a Peruvian cock-of-the-rock, a cotinga with courtship rites as outlandish as its appearance. These rituals take place in a courtship arena, where a dozen or more birds gather as dominant males prance in a series of acrobatic antics to impress the audience of drably feathered females.

Gaudy Orientals

Some of the most brilliantly colored passerines inhabit the forests of southeastern Asia. The Pekin robin (below), also called the red-billed leiothrix, is a denizen of the foothills of the Himalayas and southern China. A lively, gregarious bird, it is a member of the family of babblers, a group of some 282 highly vocal species.

The golden-fronted leafbird at right is another Oriental vocalist. Especially numerous in Malaysia, this leafbird, one of 15 species, makes its home in the topmost branches of the jungle, rarely coming to the ground. The bird's predominantly green plumage provides excellent camouflage among the leaves of the forest canopy. Traveling in pairs or small groups, golden-fronted leafbirds scour the treetops for seeds and insects. The mainstays of their diet, however, are the berries of the Oriental mistletoe and the nectar of flowers. The leafbirds are ranked among the most important "flower birds," highly active in pollinating many kinds of tropical plants.

The Pekin robin at left is a favorite
cage bird because of its lovely colors
and its cheery song. It is not a true
robin—like many other exotic birds, it
was given its common name by
homesick Europeans.

The golden-fronted leafbird (above)
gets its name from the golden band
bordering the black mask that covers
its face and extends down its chest.
The most widespread leafbird, it is
found from India eastward to Vietnam.

45

A spangled drongo (above) sits on a
dead branch where it can keep an alert
eye out for insects. The spangled
drongo is a native of Australia. The
other 19 species of drongos live in
western and southern Africa and
in Asia.

Padda oryzivora, the scientific name of
the boldly marked Java sparrow
(right), means "paddy-field rice-eater,"
referring to the bird's reputation as an
agricultural pest. A member of the
waxbill family, the Java sparrow once
had an island habitat limited to Java
and Bali but now has extended its
range throughout much of Asia.

The handsome Asian fairy bluebird (left) is a sociable, fruit-eating creature. Although they are not considered a migratory species, these fairy bluebirds, whose range extends from southwestern China to Vietnam, do travel widely in search of ripe fruit. It is not uncommon to see noisy flocks weighing down the branches of a fruit-laden wild fig tree.

Its elegant mourning suit of sleek black plumes and drooping tail feathers probably accounts for the name of Jackson's widowbird. Ironically, it is only the male of the species (below) that wears widow's weeds; the female is dressed in buff-colored feathers. Jackson's widowbirds are found in Kenya and Tanzania, where flocks roost among reeds or tall grasses and forage for insects and seeds. In courtship dances, males leap over two feet into the air.

The diamond firetail finch (right), one of the waxbills, is splendidly marked with scarlet tail coverts and splashes of white on its slate-gray wings. The firetail's short, stout, conical beak, a bold stroke of red in the middle of its snow-white face, is perfectly suited to its principal diet of grass seeds. At times when seeds are scarce, the bird also eats such insects as ants and termites. The diamond firetail inhabits the woodlands and grasslands of southern Australia.

The metallic sheen that washes over the feathers of the scarlet-chested sunbird of southern Africa (left) makes the plumes seem to shimmer in the sunlight. Sunbirds are considered the Old World equivalents of hummingbirds, although the two families are unrelated. Sunbirds have many adaptations for life among flowers, including rounded wings that allow them to flit from blossom to blossom, and a tubular tongue and slender, curving bill for easy access to the nectar they feed on.

The South Country

by Edward Thomas

Edward Thomas spent his life in poverty. In the face of his father's opposition, he left his native Wales at the age of 19 and went to London, where he pursued his ambition to become a writer. Thomas became a prolific "hack," turning out at least one book a year. But his true interest lay in another kind of writing, and along with his commercial bread-and-butter books Thomas wrote affectingly on the natural world. The South Country, *describing the countryside and inhabitants of southern England, was published in 1909. In the following excerpt from that book Thomas describes the beautiful song of the nightingale.*

One morning, very early, when the moon has not set and all the fields are cold and dewy and the woods are still massed and harbouring the night, though a few thorns stand out from their edge in affrighted virgin green, and dim starry thickets sigh a moment and are still, suddenly the silence of the chalky lane is riven and changed into a song. First, it is a fierce impetuous downfall of one clear note repeated rapidly and ending wilfully in mid-burst. Then it is a full-brimmed expectant silence passing into a long ascendant wail, and almost without intervals another and another, which has hardly ceased when it is dashed out of memory by the downpour of those rapidly repeated notes, their abrupt end and the succeeding silence. The swift notes are each as rounded and as full of liquid sweetness as a grape.

And they are clustered like the grape. But they are wild and pure as mountain water in the dawn. They are also like steel for coldness and penetration. And their onset is like nothing else; it is the nightingale's.

The long wail is like a shooting star: even as that grows out of the darkness and draws a silver line and is no more, so this glides out of the silence and curves and is no more. And yet it does not die, nor does that liquid onset. They and their ghosts people each hanging leaf in the hazel thicket so that the silence is closely stored. Other notes are shut in the pink anemone, in the white stitchwort under and about the hazels, and in the drops of dew that begin to glister in the dawn.

Beautiful as the notes are for their quality and order, it is their inhumanity that gives them their utmost fascination, the mysterious sense which they bear to us that earth is something more than a human estate, that there are things not human yet of great honour and power in the world.

The very first rush and the following wail empty the brain of what is merely human and leave only what is related to the height and depth of the whole world. Here for this hour we are remote from the parochialism of humanity. The bird has admitted a larger air. We breathe deeply of it and are made free citizens of eternity. We hear voices that were not dreamed of before, the voices of those spirits that live in minute forms of life, the spirits that weave the frost flower on the fallen branch, the gnomes of underground, those who care for the fungus on the beech root, the lichen on the trunk, the algae on the gravestone. This hazel lane is a palace of strange pomp in an empire of which we suddenly find ourselves guests, not wholly alien nor ill at ease, though the language is new. Drink but a little draught of this air and no need is there to fear the ways of men, their mockery, their cruelty, their foreignness.

The song rules the cloudy dawn, the waiting ranges of hills and their woods full of shadows yet crested with gold, their lawns of light, the soft distended grey clouds all over the sky through which the white sun looks on the world and is glad. But it has ceased when the perpendicular shafts of rain divide the mists over the hillside woods and the pewits tangle their flight through the air that is now alive with the moist gleaming of myriads of leaves on bramble, thorn and elder.

Territory and Courtship

In most temperate parts of the world, the songbird's lyric springtime tune has a romantic overtone that suggests a wandering troubadour heralding the returning sun. The actual image is more prosaic. Likely as not the soloist is an immigrant homesteader warning all potential claim jumpers to keep out. The settler is usually a lone male starting the breeding cycle by staking out enough land to feed his future family. In the case of the meadowlark, the initial territory claimed may be upward of 22 acres. But the majority of songbirds claim no more than an acre or less.

Most songbirds generally start their territorial quest in early spring when the insect population is just beginning to rise. Among the exceptions is the American goldfinch, which, when it migrates at all, arrives in Canadian meadows from southern wintering grounds as early as April but waits until August, when the thistles his young will eat are in full bloom, before signaling his claim with a sweet, high-pitched song. By contrast, the crossbill, whose family food needs are supplied by pine or spruce seeds, may proclaim his eminent domain any time the cones are abundant—as early as January or as late as August.

Once ensconced in his territory, a songbird patrols it along established paths, stopping at selected perches to cry out his ownership. Although jays are notorious for noisily attacking squirrels and other potential egg eaters, and kingbirds got their name from their fearless driving away of hawks and eagles, most passerines are concerned only with keeping out other males of their own species. In this the settler is nearly unbeatable; few of his kinsmen will even bother to challenge his property rights. Serious fighting is rare even in the border skirmishes that occur when a late-arriving male attempts to carve out an enclave of his own between the established territories of others. Displays of fluffed feathers and vocal exchanges of threats usually establish a new, revised boundary without resort to combat. Yet the instinct to attack a threatening trespasser is so ingrained that birds often smash into windows pursuing their own reflections. And in experiments they have been observed viciously pouncing on the stuffed skin of a rival.

A few days or even a few weeks after staking his claim, a songbird usually encounters an intruder that ignores his threats, neither retreating nor resisting. This is the behavior of a female. Suddenly the aggressive defender is transformed into an ardent suitor. His courtship may be as simple as that of the American robin, which does little more than serenade his mate. But most birds accompany their love songs with ritual displays. Assuming an erect posture, they ruffle their crowns, puff up their bibs and backs and fan their tails to show off their plumage, which is brightest in breeding season. Often they prance or bound about. Some even bob around like wind-up toys. And a few, such as the meadowlark and the bobolink, treat their prospective mates to a display of aerial acrobatics.

The object of such attentions may respond with indifference, flying off to look for a more desirable mate; she nearly always makes the final decision. But more often she reacts by trilling sweetly, assuming a submissive posture or engaging in antiphonal singing with her new beau. Sometimes the courting pair appears to be kissing by rubbing bills together. But this is usually a prelude to another common ritual—the feeding of the female by the male. And some females, such as the European robin, go so far as to beg for the morsels, squawking and trembling like a nestling.

In tropical and subtropical regions, some passerines take an entirely different approach to both territory and courtship. Here, where food is more abundant, there is less need to establish territories other than small areas for courting and nesting. As a result, the males are free to devote much of their time to stagecraft and to putting on some of the most spectacular courtship performances in the animal kingdom. Often the displays are communal, like those of the tiny, brightly plumaged manakins of the rain forests of Central and South America. During breeding season, male yellow-thighed manakins gather together high in the branches of the forest. They dart back and forth from perch to perch, calling and loudly snapping their wings to attract females. At each stopping point they sway to and fro and swiftly run up and down the branch, constantly stretching to show off their lemon-colored legs.

In comparable ways, the highly vocal Australian lyrebird and the brilliantly plumed, crested Peruvian cock-of-the-rock are equally adept showmen. And in the remote mountains of New Guinea, the blue bird of paradise, an opulently clad relative of the homely crow, gives one of the most extravagant performances in the bird kingdom. The routine is highly gymnastic. Like a graceful competitor on the parallel bars, the bird of paradise slowly topples over backward from his perch and swings upside down while languorously waving his long, silky flank feathers.

Male grackles in courtship display

The Sound of Music

Apart from the purely esthetic pleasure they provide, recordings of birdsongs are an important source of scientific information about avian communication and behavior. The first known recording of a birdsong was made in Germany in 1889, but it was not until after World War II, with the invention of magnetic tape and sophisticated portable field equipment, that completely accurate transcriptions could be made. Another enormous advance was the invention of the audiospectrograph, which produces "pictures," called sonograms (right, top), accurate visual representations of the sounds birds make with beaks and feet as well as the songs, often inaudible to the human ear, produced by the syrinx, a unique respiratory organ.

Among the pioneers in these sonic studies is Cornell University's Laboratory of Ornithology, with its Library of Natural Sounds, the oldest and largest collection of bird recordings in the world. "For studies of behavior and animal communications," says Cornell's Dr. James L. Gulledge (shown below recording birdsongs with a shotgun condenser microphone and a parabolic reflector), "recordings of a bird's sounds fill a role analogous to that filled by museum skins and anatomical specimens used in studies of morphology and anatomy."

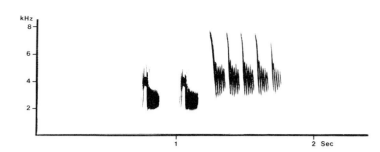

The sound frequencies in the song of a rufous-sided towhee, above, are shown precisely in a sonogram (top). Pitch is recorded in the height of the graph, loudness in the thickness, and the speed by horizontal measurement.

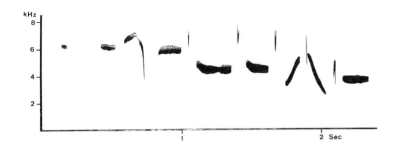

The vibrations of the notes of a tree sparrow are made visible in the pattern of lines overhead. Sonograms have been used to determine that some birds sing regional "dialects," and others must learn their family songs.

The song of the blue-winged warbler above is, like the other sonograms shown here, a territorial proclamation, sung by the male bird to warn off rivals and to affirm his right to the nesting site he has claimed.

Colors of Courtship

Some males and females belonging to the same species look so much alike that they can spot the opposite sex only by the love song of the male or the passive behavior of the female. The vivid creatures on these pages have more obvious means of recognition. The male cardinal (left) is easily distinguished from his more drably feathered mate (below), as are the flamboyant male summer tanager and olive-coated female (right, below). Bluebirds (right, above) resemble each other more closely, but if the paler female has any recognition problems, the excited fluttering and incessant warbling of the male soon convince her.

The family crest and unmistakable profile identify the cardinal as surely as its distinct coloration. In the East the cardinal was formerly native only to the area from New Jersey south, but now nests as far north as Quebec

56

Plighting his troth, a male bluebird
(above, left) seems diffident. Actually,
bluebirds are sexually precocious,
pairing off soon after fledging.

The handsome pair below are summer
tanagers, migratory members of a large
and brightly colored clan that lives
mostly in the tropics.

Riverby

by John Burroughs

In his first book, Wake-Robin *(1871), John Burroughs, the Hudson River naturalist, suggested that the study of birds brings "a new interest in the fields and woods, a new moral and intellectual tonic, a new key to the treasure house of nature." Burroughs was one of the first American nature writers to study living birds, their activities and their habitats. His careful observations and detailed descriptions are evident in the following excerpt from* Riverby, *the work of a pioneer bird watcher.*

The bluebird wins his mate by the ardor of his attentions and the sincerity of his compliments, and by finding a house ready built which cannot be surpassed. The male bluebird is usually here several days before the female, and he sounds forth his note as loudly and eloquently as he can till she appears. On her appearance he flies at once to the box or tree cavity upon which he has had his eye, and as he looks into it calls and warbles in his most persuasive tones. The female at such times is always shy and backward, and the contrast in the manners of the two birds is as striking as the contrast in their colors. The male is brilliant and ardent; the female is dim and retiring, not to say indifferent. She may take a hasty peep into the hole in the box or tree and then fly away, uttering a lonesome, homesick note. Only by a wooing of many days is she to be fully won.

The past April I was witness one Sunday morning to the jealousies that may rage in these little brown breasts. A pair of bluebirds had apparently mated and decided to occupy a woodpecker's lodge in the limb of an old apple-tree near my study. But that morning another male appeared on the scene and was bent on cutting the first male out, and carrying off his bride. I happened to be near by when the two birds came into collision. They fell to the grass and kept their grip upon each other for half a minute. Then they separated and the first up flew to the hole and called fondly to the female. This was too much for the other male and they clinched again and fell to the ground as before. There they lay upon the grass, blue and brown intermingled. But not a feather was tweaked out or even disturbed, that I could see. They simply held each other down. Then they separated again, and again rushed upon each other. The battle raged for about fifteen minutes, when one of the males, which one, of course, I could not tell, withdrew and flew to a box under the eaves of the study and exerted all the eloquence he possessed to induce the female to come to him there. How he warbled and called and lifted his wings and flew to the entrance to the box and called again! The female was evidently strongly attracted; she would respond and fly about halfway to an apple-tree and look toward him. The other male in the meantime did his best to persuade her to cast her lot with him. He followed her to the tree toward his rival, and then flew back to the nest and spread his plumage and called and warbled, oh, so confidently, so fondly, so reassuringly! When the female would return and peep into the hole in the tree what fine, joyous notes he would utter; then he would look in and twinkle his wings and say something his rival could not hear. This vocal and pantomimic contest went on for a long time. The female was evidently greatly shaken in her allegiance to the male in the old apple-tree. In less than an hour another female responded to the male who had sought the eaves of the study, and flew with him to the box. Whether this was their first meeting or not I do not know, but it was clear enough that the heart of the male was fixed upon the bride of his rival. He would devote himself a moment to the newcomer and then turn toward the old apple-tree, and call and lift his wings. Then, apparently admonished by the bird near him, would turn again to her and induce her to look into the box and warble fondly. Then up on a higher branch again, with his attention directed toward his first love, between whom and himself salutations seemed constantly passing. This little play went on for some time, when the two females came into collision, and fell to the ground tweaking each other spitefully. Then the four birds drifted away from me down into the vineyard, where the males closed with each other again and fell to the ploughed ground and lay there a surprisingly long time, nearly two minutes, as we calculated. Their wings were outspread, and their forms were indistinguishable. They tugged at each other most doggedly, one or the other brown breast was generally turned up, partly overlaid by a blue coat. They were determined to make a finish of it this time, but which got the better of the fight I could not tell. But it was the last battle; they finally separated, neither, apparently, any the worse for the encounter. The females fought two more rounds, the males looking on and warbling approvingly when they separated, and the two pairs drifted away in different directions. The next day they were about the box and tree again, and seemed to have definitely settled matters. Who won and who lost I do not know, but two pairs of bluebirds have since been very busy and very happy about the two nesting places. One of the males I recognize as a bird that appeared early in March; I recognize him from one peculiar note in the midst of his warble, a note that suggests a whistle.

Aerial Combatants

Red-winged blackbirds are among the earliest harbingers of spring. Large groups of males arrive in their swampy northern nesting grounds in late February to establish their individual territories and await the arrival of the females a few weeks later. Although they are normally gregarious birds, often living in flocks of hundreds, male redwings become belligerent defenders of territory during nesting season. As a rule, a male needs merely to flaunt his distinctive scarlet epaulets and scream out a raucous warning to scare off all but the most aggressive intruders. But in the face of a determined predator, such as a hawk or a snake, a red-winged blackbird will unhesitatingly defend his nestlings to the death.

The evening grosbeaks, beautiful golden birds of the northern pine forests, also swarm together but are much more quarrelsome at nesting time—and indeed at any time of the year—than the redwings. The feisty grosbeaks are equally as ready to fight over food as to defend their territory against intruders.

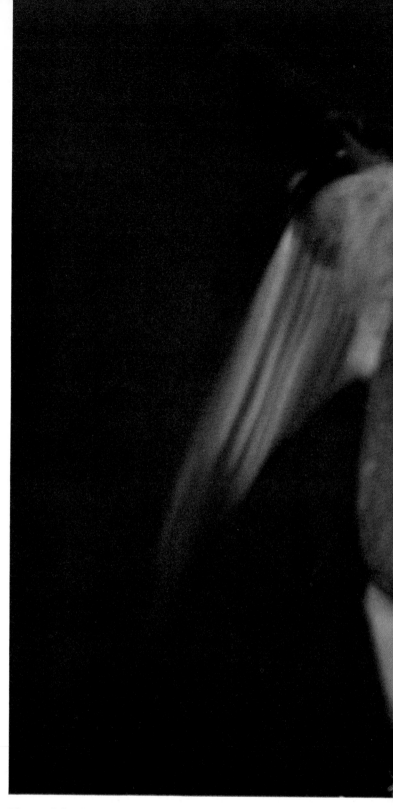

The vivid shoulder patch of the male red-winged blackbird (left) is truly a red badge of courage. In an experiment, when their epaulets were painted black the treated birds completely lost their bravado.

Two male evening grosbeaks, plumage gleaming, contest a territorial boundary. Although their name would seem to indicate that they are twilight singers, these scrappy grosbeaks are more likely to sing in the mornings, when they are most active. Their courtship is more often than not a matter of the silent display of their fine feathers alone, unaccompanied by the nuptial song characteristic of most other songbirds.

Adept and Gorgeous Wooers

When Magellan's flagship, *Victoria*, returned to Spain in 1522, it brought from the Indies the feathers of magnificent birds of New Guinea. The awestruck Spaniards decided that such glorious feathers could not possibly belong to earthly creatures and must therefore come from heaven. The resulting name ''bird of paradise'' has persisted, a name that coincides with the Malayan phrase for them, ''birds of the gods.'' The birds are collectively the most gorgeously feathered troupe in the avian world, and their fine feathers serve a sole purpose: to dazzle the modestly plumed female birds of paradise in a spectacular display of feathers that would put any parade of showgirls to shame.

Bowerbirds are also inhabitants of Australia and New Guinea. Although they, too, are often handsomely plumed, their courtship involves an entirely different but equally impressive kind of display. They woo their mates with elaborately decorated stages (pages 64–65), ''maypoles'' (opposite) or ''avenues'' of arched plants. Only two of the 19 species of bowerbirds build no love nests and rely solely on bright feathers and courtship antics to attract mates.

The ribbon-tailed bird of paradise (above) was not discovered in its New Guinea mountain fastness until 1938. Its twin tails trail three feet behind in flight and arch quiveringly overhead in courtship.

A canary-colored golden bowerbird (right) arranges a bit of lichen on its ''maypole,'' a structure that, when completed, may tower nine feet above the ground—an astonishing construction for a nine-inch bird.

Bridal Suite

The courtship pavilions erected by male bowerbirds of Australia and New Guinea are so ornate and fanciful that early explorers decided they must be the playhouses of aboriginal children, believing that no other creature but man could have such a talent for architecture and decoration. The bowers vary according to the styles of different bowerbird species and are used solely for courtship. Immediately after mating, the female turns her back on her mate and his bower and departs to lay her eggs and raise her young in a simple nursery nest she builds alone.

A great gray bowerbird adds a bright bottle cap to the decor of his nuptial stage (left). Other decorations intended to attract a reluctant mate are bones, snail shells and an orchid. Above, a great gray arranges the pebbles in front of his bower.

Love Stories

The ways of courtship among birds involve dozens of peculiar rituals, from aerial displays and intertwined bills to trilled love songs and invitations to painted bridal suites. In those species where the male plays a role in the care and feeding of the young, courtship often ends with the ceremonial feeding of the female, a prelude to the time when the male will bring her food—and help sustain her strength—while she is brooding her eggs, and later help her to feed the insatiable nestlings. The house finches at right—also called linnets—perform the courtship rite with the female sometimes begging and crying like a fledgling and the male offering her a seed much as a human swain might present a candy to his lady love.

Another act of courtship is demonstrated by the pair of white-crested laughing thrushes below, indulging in mutual preening, a prerequisite to mating among these small ground-feeding birds, inhabitants of the mountain forests of eastern Asia.

Laughing thrushes (above) travel together in large groups and communicate with one another by a call that sounds eerily like human laughter. House finches (right) are also sociable, flocking together except in breeding season, and are noted for their exceptionally sweet song.

66

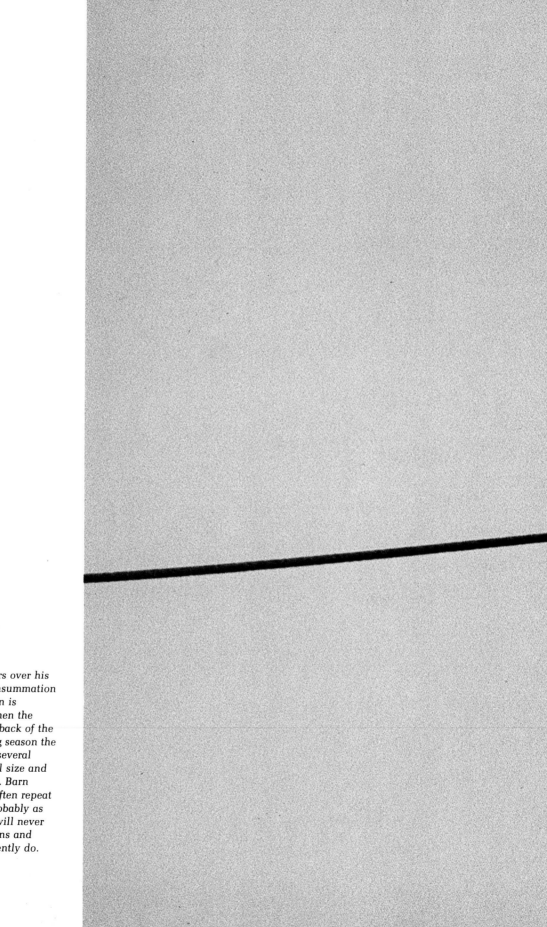

A male barn swallow hovers over his mate (right) in the final consummation of his courtship. Copulation is achieved moments later when the male alights briefly on the back of the female. During the breeding season the male bird's testes swell to several hundred times their normal size and shrink again after breeding. Barn swallows and other birds often repeat copulation many times, probably as insurance that the female will never lay infertile eggs, as chickens and other domestic fowls frequently do.

68

Birds on the Western Front

by H. H. Munro

Born in Burma in 1870, H. H. Munro was raised in England by two cruel and oppressive aunts. That bleak childhood served as a fine background for the ironic and piquant studies of upper-class English relationships that Munro wrote under the pen name of "Saki." Munro enlisted in the British army at the outset of the first World War in 1914 and was killed in France two years later. His wartime writings include Birds on the Western Front, *an ironic account of the effect of "the war to end all wars" on the lives of the birds in a battlefield in northern France.*

Apart from the owls one cannot notice that the campaign is making any marked difference in the bird life of the country-side. The vast flocks of crows and ravens that one expected to find in the neighbourhood of the fighting line are nonexistent, which is perhaps rather a pity. The obvious explanation is that the roar and crash and fumes of high explosives have driven the crow tribe in panic from the fighting area; like many obvious explanations, it is not a correct one. The crows of the locality are not attracted to the battlefield, but they certainly are not scared away from it. The rook is normally so gun-shy and nervous where noise is concerned that the sharp banging of a barn door or the report of a toy pistol will sometimes set an entire rookery in commotion; out here I have seen him sedately busy among the refuse heaps of a battered village, with shells bursting at no great distance, and the impatient-sounding, snapping rattle of machine-guns going on all round him; for all the notice that he took he might have been in some peaceful English meadow on a sleepy Sunday afternoon. Whatever else German frightfulness may have done it has not frightened the rook of North-Eastern France; it has made his nerves steadier than they have ever

been before, and future generations of small boys, employed in scaring rooks away from the sown crops in this region, will have to invent something in the way of super-frightfulness to achieve their purpose. Crows and magpies are nesting well within the shell-swept area, and over a small beech-copse I once saw a pair of crows engaged in hot combat with a pair of sparrow-hawks, while considerably higher in the sky, but almost directly above them, two Allied battle-planes were engaging an equal number of enemy aircraft.

Unlike the barn owls, the magpies have had their choice of building sites considerably restricted by the ravages of war; the whole avenues of poplars, where they were accustomed to construct their nests, have been blown to bits, leaving nothing but dreary-looking rows of shattered and splintered trunks to show where once they stood. Affection for a particular tree has in one case induced a pair of magpies to build their bulky, domed nest in the battered remnants of a poplar of which so little remained standing that the nest looked almost bigger than the tree; the effect rather suggested an archiepiscopal enthronement taking

place in the ruined remains of Melrose Abbey. The magpie, wary and suspicious in his wild state, must be rather intrigued at the change that has come over the erstwhile fearsome, not-to-be-avoided human, stalking everywhere over the earth as its possessor, who now creeps about in screened and sheltered ways, as chary of showing himself in the open as the shyest of wild creatures.

The buzzard, that earnest seeker after mice, does not seem to be taking any war risks, at least I have never seen one out here, but kestrels hover about all day in the hottest parts of the line, not in the least disconcerted, apparently, when a promising mouse-area suddenly rises in the air in a cascade of black or yellow earth. Sparrow-hawks are fairly numerous, and a mile or two back from the firing line I saw a pair of hawks that I took to be red-legged falcons, circling over the top of an oak-copse. According to investigations made by Russian naturalists, the effect of the war on bird life on the Eastern front has been more marked than it has been over here. "During the first year of the war rooks disappeared, larks no longer sang in the fields, the wild pigeon disappeared also." The skylark in this region

has stuck tenaciously to the meadows and crop-lands that have been seamed and bisected with trenches and honeycombed with shell-holes. In the chill, misty hour of gloom that precedes a rainy dawn, when nothing seemed alive except a few wary waterlogged sentries and many scuttling rats, the lark would suddenly dash skyward and pour forth a song of ecstatic jubilation that sounded horribly forced and insincere. It seemed scarcely possible that the bird could carry its insouciance to the length of attempting to rear a brood in that desolate wreckage of shattered clods and gaping shellholes, but once, having occasion to throw myself down with some abruptness on my face, I found myself nearly on the top of a brood of young larks. Two of them had already been hit by something, and were in rather a battered condition, but the survivors seemed as tranquil and comfortable as the average nestling.

At the corner of a stricken wood (which has had a name made for it in history, but shall be nameless here), at a moment when lyddite and shrapnel and machine-gun fire

72

swept and raked and bespattered that devoted spot as though the artillery of an entire Division had suddenly concentrated on it, a wee hen-chaffinch flitted wistfully to and fro, amid splintered and falling branches that had never a green bough left on them. The wounded lying there, if any of them noticed the small bird, may well have wondered why anything having wings and no pressing reason for remaining should have chosen to stay in such a place. There was a battered orchard alongside the stricken wood, and the probable explanation of the bird's presence was that it had a nest of young ones whom it was too scared to feed, too loyal to desert. Later on, a small flock of chaffinches blundered into the wood, which they were doubtless in the habit of using as a highway to their feeding-grounds; unlike the solitary hen-bird, they made no secret of their desire to get away as fast as their dazed wits would let them. The only other bird I ever saw there was a magpie, flying low over the wreckage of fallen tree-limbs; "one for sorrow," says the old superstition. There was sorrow enough in that wood.

Nesting

Once the brief rites of courtship end, most songbirds have only a few days—or weeks at most—before their eggs are laid, and they immediately set about the task of providing shelter for their incipient offspring. House sparrows and starlings sometimes solve the problem by simply expropriating the holes used by other birds, forcibly evicting the rightful owner. Even before courtship, bluebirds, titmice and other hole nesters usually locate an abandoned woodpecker's hole, although they still have quite a lot of work to do refurbishing the woodpecker's spartan quarters with a bed of comfortable nesting material.

The nursery that most passerines build for their young, however, is the familiar cup-shaped nest—and usually it is well crafted. Even the loose tangle of sticks thrown together by the common crow has a plush lining of hair, shredded bark or leaves. At the other extreme, the deep cup of the American goldfinch—a weave of moss and fine grass lined with feltlike thistledown—is so tightly knit that it will hold water and drown the young if a heavy rain should fall while the parents are away from the nest.

The nest of the American robin is one example of superb craftsmanship. On a sturdy limb—often in a fork or a crook near the trunk—the female robin, aided by her mate, fashions a platform of interlaced twigs, coarse grass and rootlets. Her weight tamps down the center as she settles and turns, tucking and pulling with her bill to build up the outer rim. Then, continuing to turn round and round to shape the material with her breast, she adds a layer of mud and finishes with a mattress of feathers and fine grass.

Like the robin, most other songbirds find trees the safest sites for their constructions, usually from six to eight feet above the ground—high enough to be out of the reach of most terrestrial predators but still sheltered from rain and sun by the tree's canopy. For added protection against predators, including such airborne enemies as hawks, some tree nesters tack bits of lichen to their cups as camouflage. Obviously, birds that build on or near the ground take the greatest care to hide their nests. Meadowlarks weave a domed roof out of growing grass stems, and some warblers erect an arch of weed stalks and dead leaves.

Almost any pliable material may end up in a passerine's nest. In the South, a bird may add some Spanish moss. In coniferous forests, needles are certain to be included. A swamp-dwelling blackbird uses waterlogged reeds and grass that tighten into a sturdy basket as they dry. And near human habitations, bits of cloth, paper and string are common nesting materials.

Mud is a key foundation for the nests of some songbirds. Barn swallows alternate pellets of wet mud with straw to form their roomy bowls, then line them with soft feathers; their cousins, the cliff swallows, use almost nothing but mud for the earthen jugs that they fasten under ledges, eaves and bridges, often in colonies of a hundred or more. The master mason, however, is the rufous ovenbird of South America, which mixes wet soil with cow dung and then, a beakful at a time, shapes the mixture into a hard foot-high ball complete with a main chamber and a separate vestibule just inside the entrance. In Argentina, where it is the national bird, the ovenbird is known as *el hornero*, the baker, and its mud ovens are a common sight on the pampas, where they dot the branches of the sparse trees as well as telephone poles and fenceposts.

Even more impressive examples of avian architecture are the suspended nests of some passerines. The tiny hanging baskets of the vireos are secured only by their rims to the fork of a bough. And the pendulous pouches of the orioles, which are sometimes as much as 18 inches deep, often sag from the slender tip of an upper branch. Although such nests seem precarious, they are actually very well engineered. The hanging nests constructed by the Eurasian penduline tit are so well knit that they used to be worn by Eastern European children as slippers.

The most accomplished nest builders in the world are the weaverbirds of Africa and southern Asia, whose large globe-shaped baskets dangle from a thin cord. Tiny and sparrowlike, these birds actually tie knots to secure their cords to the tree and earn their name by plaiting fibers from palms and banana trees into an intricate basketwork on a pattern close to the warp and woof produced by a loom.

Less carefully crafted, the nest of the social weavers, the South African members of the weaverbird family, is a gigantic group-effort construction. Often measuring over 12 feet in both diameter and height, the nest looks like a haystack inadvertently deposited in a tree—usually a solitary acacia on the veld. A thatched roof as watertight as that of an English cottage shelters nesting chambers for as many as 125 pairs of birds, each with its own private entry. Repaired and enlarged each year, some of these avian apartment houses last for more than a century before the supporting branches finally give way under the weight.

A golden palm weaver finishing a nest

Homespun Housing

The nesting sites of weavers, a predominantly African family that includes the black-headed weaver (right) and the golden palm weaver (below), are scenes of extraordinary activity in the breeding season. Weavers are sociable birds, living together in colonies that may number 100 nests, slung from branches or palm fronds only a foot or so apart.

For male weavers, nest building is a part of sexual display, and when breeding season is at hand they begin collecting strips of fresh green vegetable matter that they braid into intricate patterns, employing a variety of knots and bows. The finished nest is a globular affair, stiff and sturdy once the green strips dry out. It has an entrance at the bottom and is often finished off with a dangling, woven entrance tunnel several inches long. The male weaver hangs from the bottom, chirping and fluttering his wings to attract a female. Once he succeeds, he mates with her and leaves her in the love nest while he repeats the process, building four or five nests in a single breeding season.

A golden palm weaver, wrapped up in his work, begins constructing a nest (left). Because a weaver's toes are so dexterous, he can hold a loop of fiber with one foot, pulling more fiber through with the other to form a knot.

A black-headed weaver (above)
completes the first stage of his nest—a
ring of fibers to perch on while he
finishes the nest. Weavers are in a
minority of bird species where nest
building is left to the males.

Like ornaments decorating a Christmas tree, weaver nests dot a palm tree in Mozambique (above). Half-finished nests are a common sight, abandoned by male weavers whose mating urge cooled during construction.

Weaver nests, some with entrance tunnels and some without, are visible in the picture at right. These nests were built by one of the few Asian species of weavers. Besides tunnel entrances, the ingenious weavers have developed other techniques to protect their eggs and young from predators. To make nests less accessible and to repel predators, they frequently build in trees overhanging water or near bees, wasps or even humans.

Cliff swallows gather mud for homemaking (above). These forays are about the only time they ever come to earth, for the birds are as awkward on the ground as they are graceful in the air. In dry periods or in areas with no mud, cliff swallows make their own, standing first in water, then moving to dusty soil and mixing it with the moisture on their feet.

Cliff swallow nests adorn a rock face in the Colorado Rockies (right). Swallows often return to the same cliff nest year after year, until the mud of the nest crumbles. The nests of house- or barn-dwelling swallows, however, are often usurped by house sparrows when the swallows fly south.

The Cliff Dwellers

When the swallows come back to Capistrano, where exactly have they come from? The birds in question are cliff swallows, and they are returning from a winter migration deep into South America, a remarkable trip for birds only five or six inches long. The first thing cliff swallows do upon returning to their summer range, which extends from Alaska to Nova Scotia and south to Central America, is to search out a good mudhole near their chosen nesting site (left). Mud is the material they use to construct the gourd-shaped nests with entrances at the neck (below).

A male and a female work together, making hundreds of trips from mudhole to nest, painstakingly carrying a tiny pellet of mud rolled in their beak on each trip. Rocky ledges are the cliff swallows' natural nesting sites, but with man's encroachment on their range, the birds will settle for the side of a tall building, a house in the city or the eaves of a barn in the country.

Designs for Living

Though many passerines are difficult to tell apart at a glance, each species constructs such an individual nest that the building materials, combined with location, shape and size, usually establish identification of the owner. Despite this diversity, all nests share one characteristic: They are designed so as to afford protection for the eggs—and later the young. The northern oriole, for example, usually weaves its hanging nest at the very end of a drooping bough (far right), high over water or even a busy highway and often so inaccessible that even tree snakes have been observed falling while trying to approach an oriole nest. The pardalote (below), a small Australian bird, burrows into the side of a riverbank to deposit its eggs safely out of any predator's way.

Helmet-shrikes, members of an African subfamily of shrikes, camouflage their nests with cobwebs and bits of lichen (right). As many as four or five birds will work together to collect the vegetable fiber and grass that go into the neat, bark-lined cup nest.

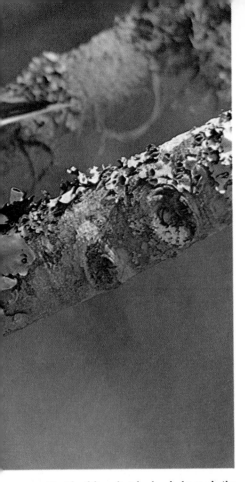

Nest building finished, a helmet-shrike incubates eggs atop its camouflaged nest (above). Although most shrikes are aggressive, carnivorous birds that prey on small mammals, reptiles and other birds, helmet-shrikes are sociable, insect-eating creatures that work and nest in groups.

Master builder among birds, a northern oriole with a mouthful of food prepares to feed her chicks (right). The nest, an intricately woven affair of moss, plant fibers, hair and bits of string, can be spotted throughout the bird's breeding range—from southern Canada to Mexico.

A black-headed pardalote (left) pulls up sharply in front of its nest—a tunnel that it and a mate excavated for raising their young. Known as the diamondbird in its native Australia, the pardalote feeds almost exclusively on insects and their larvae.

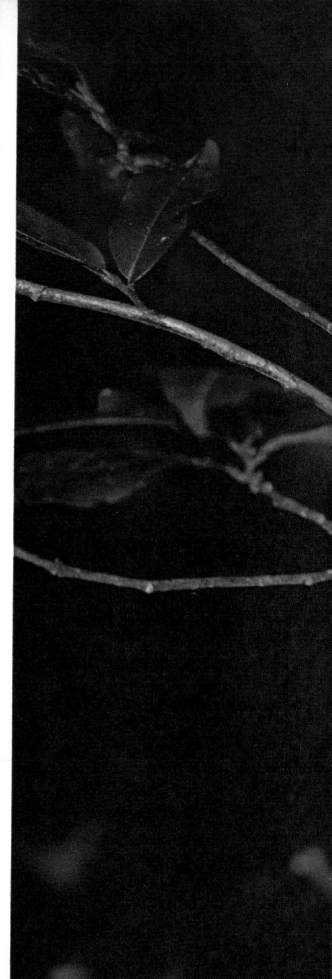

Squeezing through a knothole opening in the side of a barn, an English (or house) sparrow leaves the nest it has built just inside. From several pairs of sparrows imported to the United States around 1850, the hardy, adaptable bird spread within 50 years to almost every part of North America.

A rufous-backed fantail sits atop its wineglass-shaped nest of moss, rootlets, grass, bark, lichens and cobwebs. Ranging through Australia, New Zealand and New Guinea, the insectivorous birds almost always breed near water, where they can find ample food.

Audubon's Eggs

The paintings of eggs on these pages are part of a group of watercolors by the Haitian-born artist and naturalist John James Audubon, painted during 1829, one of the most productive years of his life. From May to August of that

Song sparrow

Ovenbird

Purple grackle

Field sparrow

Marsh wren

Vesper sparrow

year, Audubon traveled throughout the northeastern United States and completed watercolors and drawings of more than 60 eggs and 95 birds. The paintings demonstrate the ecological function of egg coloring: Ground nesters nearly always produce spotted eggs that blend in well with the area around the nest, while tree or bush nesters often lay eggs with a bluish or greenish background so that the eggs are less visible in the uneven light in foliage.

Hermit thrush

Cowbird

Yellow-breasted chat

Scarlet tanager

Sharp-tailed sparrow

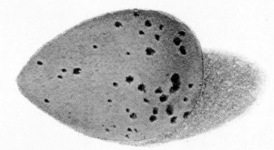

Yellow-throated vireo

Raising Young

Songbirds are among the most indefatigable parents in the animal kingdom. The female shows remarkable stamina just in the act of producing her clutch of eggs. In rare cases, like that of the prolific European great tit, the clutch may exceed the weight of her own tiny body, numbering as many as 20 eggs. Even the American robin's more typical clutch of four, each egg laid a day apart, requires considerable physical endurance. Before the eggs are laid, the future mother undergoes a physiological transformation for brooding by losing all the downy feathers on her breast so that her warm skin will be in direct contact with the eggs. And as the time for incubation approaches, an increased flow of blood to the naked spot raises the surface temperature to an even higher level.

Under the warming breast of its parent, the embryonic chick develops rapidly in the egg. In about two weeks' time, it absorbs all of the white and most of the yolk. Soon the unhatched chick begins to breathe air seeping through the porous shell and even starts to peep weakly. Its neck muscles become unusually strong, and it sprouts a hard temporary growth called an egg tooth on the tip of its upper bill. And when the time finally comes to hatch, the chick uses the egg tooth to chip away at the confining walls—first cracking the shell, then breaking it in half and struggling out, wet and wobbly, into the world.

Unlike hatchlings among many other orders of birds, which leave the egg feathered and alert, the newly hatched songbird is a feeble creature—naked, eyes closed and so utterly helpless that it needs almost constant parental attention. After quickly clearing away the odoriferous fragments of shell, which might attract predators and insects to the nest (only a few songbirds, such as goldfinches, tolerate messy nests), adult songbirds continue to brood the hatchlings, covering them with body and wings, since the young emerge cold-blooded and are at first unable to regulate their own body temperature. During this period the chicks are so weak that they may have to be encouraged to eat. But soon they begin to gape and squawk for food whenever the returning parent jiggles the nest.

At this early point in its life, a baby songbird is mostly mouth—an oversized, gleaming cavern, often brightly colored in red, orange or yellow, that serves as a convenient and recognizable target for the foraging parent, which quickly thrusts its food-laden beak deep down into the nestling's throat. In the early morning, when feeding is most intense, 25 or more food-gathering trips an hour are common, and the large broods of some titmice are fed as frequently as once a minute. The pace slackens toward noon and resumes again late in the afternoon, but hardly an hour of daylight goes by without some food being brought to the nest. In one careful tabulation, the day's total for a great tit proved to be close to a thousand trips for fast food.

In the first days after hatching the father is more often than not the chief forager, while the mother is brooding her young. Whenever it is fed, the chick usually responds by turning around, raising its rump and delivering a neatly packaged sack of waste to the parent, which promptly swallows it or carries it away.

In from three to five days, the nestlings' eyes open, and within another day or two, midway during the nesting period, downy feathers begin to appear all over their bodies. With this insulation they need to be brooded only at night, and the mother is able to join in the quest for food. Soon the nestlings become much more active; in open nests they stretch and test their wings. And, among smaller species, usually only two weeks after hatching, they are ready to fledge. For most songbirds the first flight is a fluttering, uncertain hop to a nearby branch. But many hole-nesters, like the bank swallow, though they have never even had a chance to exercise their wings, make astonishingly strong and well-coordinated first flights. Most songbirds continue to feed and watch over their fledglings until they are able to care for themselves. In some species, such as the American robin, the father takes charge of the newly fledged family, while the mother flies off to raise another brood before the chill of autumn sets in.

In their constant rounds of frantic activity, parent songbirds are not always alone. Sometimes they are aided by their young from a brood that hatched earlier that season or even the year before. Sometimes unmated males attach themselves to a mated pair, helping them feed and raise their young. And among certain highly social birds, including the piñon jay of the American Southwest, breeding pairs help other pairs feed nestlings and fledglings. As Alexander Scutch, a noted ornithologist who has spent much of his long career studying nesting habits, observes: "One of the reasons why passerine birds have covered the earth is the perfection of their parental instincts, which ensure not only the best care of their own offspring but also tenderness toward their neighbors' young."

European goldfinches caring for nestlings

Breakfast in Bed

Wood warblers are a strictly American family of 120 species, including Wilson's warbler (below) and the American redstart (right). While nest building among warblers is occasionally shared by both male and female, incubation of the eggs is solely a female task. As shown on these pages, the male sometimes feeds his mate as she sits on the eggs, but usually she provides her own food.

Thus there are periods when the nest is left uncovered while the mother bird goes off to feed. In passerines whose food sources are generally abundant and readily available, such absences may amount to no more than a few minutes every hour or half hour and usually have no adverse effect on the embryo in the egg. Although the development of the embryo is suspended when the temperature of the egg drops to 82° F. or less, it can withstand extended periods at lower temperatures and still survive to hatch.

A male Wilson's warbler (above) perches on the edge of his bowl-like nest and attentively feeds his incubating mate. The birds are named for ornithologist Alexander Wilson.

As the female consumes an insect while she broods her clutch of eggs (right), a male American redstart stands by with a second helping held firmly in his bill.

The day-old house wrens at right sit surrounded by the speckled shells of their soon-to-be-hatched siblings. The youngsters are born sightless and remain so until they are about three days old, when their eyes open. Soon after hatching, they begin to beg raucously for food. Like all young passerines, the six-day-old house wrens below have brightly colored mouth linings. These gaping saffron orifices tell their parents exactly where to drop the food they bring back to the nest. One pair of house wrens was observed to have made 600 food-gathering trips in a single day.

Open Wide

Among the most familiar of the passerines are the house wrens, found from Tierra del Fuego in South America to as far north as southern Canada. The four- to five-inch dappled, round-bodied birds lay clutches that vary in size from five to eight eggs and usually produce two separate clutches each season. The female house wren takes full responsibility for her eggs during the 12- to 15-day incubation period. But once the young are hatched, both parents share the arduous job of finding enough insects to feed their insatiable offspring.

Young house wrens have a nest life of between 12 and 18 days, depending on the size of the brood and the availability of food. At the age of about a week juvenile feathers appear, and the nestlings begin stretching and strengthening their wings in preparation for the day they will leave the nest. House wren males continue feeding the fledglings for a few days after they have left the nest, freeing the females, who thereupon depart to lay a new clutch of eggs in another nest and begin the life cycle again before the end of summer.

Food Cooperative

Among many passerines rearing the young is often a two-parent job, and the quartet on these pages is an example of that cooperation. The scissor-tailed male paradise fly-catcher of Africa (left) does his share of the incubating and feeding of the nestlings, an unusual trait in such a strikingly marked bird—flamboyantly plumed males seldom act a parental role. Male and female barn swallows (below) share the chores of the incubation of their eggs and the nurture of the nestlings. The male stays briefly with the young after they leave the nest, teaching them to forage for insects while the female goes off to lay a new clutch.

Like most groups of birds in which the sexes look alike, red-eyed vireo males (bottom) take part in incubating their eggs—or those of interloping cowbirds—and then assume most of the responsibility for feeding the young. Parent starlings take turns feeding the nestlings (opposite).

A barn swallow approaches its hungry brood (above). When the nestlings are about three weeks old they are encouraged to leave the nest by a parent that flies just beyond their reach with food in its bill.

A handsome paradise flycatcher sits protectively by its young (above). These forest-dwelling birds range from Africa to Japan and feed exclusively on insects.

A red-eyed vireo (left) looks into the
begging mouths of a brood made up
solely of cowbirds, which parasitize
nests of vireos, replacing the vireo eggs
with their own.

A European starling hovers in the air
as it deposits a morsel into the mouth
of one of its young (above). Starlings
were introduced into the United States
from England in 1890–91.

Helpmate

Orioles are a songbird group of about 30 species found throughout the New World. Like most other members of the clan, the female northern oriole assumes almost all of the burden of raising the young, although, as shown on these pages, the male assists in the feeding. Dressed in a relatively somber plumage in shades of yellow, green and white, the female makes repeated food-gathering forays into the woods for her hungry brood, while her more flamboyantly colored black-and-gold mate zealously guards the nest from such predators as squirrels and jays.

The English word "oriole" derives from the Latin word *aureolus*, meaning yellow or golden, and refers to the characteristic shades in the plumage of all these birds. The northern oriole is perhaps the best known of all the orioles. The name is the designation recently given to both the familiar Baltimore oriole and Bullock's oriole. Once considered separate species, the two have been reclassified as one because they are now known to interbreed.

In this sequence of pictures, a male northern oriole is seen delivering a stick insect to his demanding offspring (above), which quickly takes it (right) and polishes it off (far right). Orioles will also sip nectar from flowers.

A quintet of fledgling crows huddles
on a branch awaiting the arrival of
their parents and their next meal.
Crows are social creatures, and the
members of a brood get along quite
amiably. Even when all the young
birds are begging for food there is
rarely any attempt by one chick to
steal a morsel from another. Thievery
is further discouraged by the fact that
the parent bird thrusts food so far
down into the gullet of its eager
recipient that a rival fledgling could
not possibly retrieve it.

98

Feeding

From the robin locating worm after worm by a method of sounding that baffles ornithologists, to the towhee's noisy rustling as it hops around and rapidly scratches the forest floor with both feet, foraging for food is the principal activity of any songbird. With their small bodies and high metabolic rate, most passerines must consume the equivalent of 10 percent of their body weight every day in order to survive. Each species has evolved its own characteristic way of meeting that need.

Jays, ravens and most other members of the crow family will eat almost anything—small mammals, other birds, eggs, frogs, snakes and snails, as well as grain and fruit. Some even join vultures in scavenging on carrion. And a few that live near water feed on fish or clams. Though many other songbirds have a less indiscriminate menu of favored foods, whether meat or vegetable, they are quite willing to vary their diet with the environment or season. Insect-eating thrushes and orioles, for example, often harvest ripe fruit in summer just as robins gorge on cherries.

Other passerines follow a much stricter regimen, and usually such specialists are anatomically well adapted for their eating habits. This is especially true among the birds that feed primarily on grain and nuts. Sparrows, finches and other seed eaters have small, stout beaks that allow them to slice the hard edge off a kernel before swallowing it. The hawfinch has a bill constructed to exert considerable force, with bones and muscles so powerful that it has won the admiration of engineers. Weighing only a scant two ounces, a hawfinch can exert a force of up to 150 pounds to crack the stone of a cherry or the pit of an olive. The most remarkable adaptation among seed eaters is the beak of the crossbill. As its name indicates, the tips of its bill are uniquely crossed, and the divergence of the tips enables the odd bird to lever apart the scales of pine cones and easily extract the seeds.

The bills of insectivorous passerines are also well suited to their task. Swallows and flycatchers have wide, gaping beaks like scoops that trap flying prey, and some species are equipped with bristle-fringed bills that may act like nets. On the ground, songbirds that probe for insects have appropriately long, thin beaks. Like the starling, most of these birds use their needlelike bills to explore holes in the earth, but some, the woodcreepers for example, cling to the sides of trees, poking their long, tapering beaks into the cracks and crevices in the bark, sometimes excavating holes in the manner of woodpeckers to get at insects. Some members of this family, aptly named scythebills, have a slender, sharply curved, three-inch-long beak resembling a grappling hook.

For one tree-probing passerine, the woodpecker finch of the Galápagos Islands, a blunt bill would seem to be a handicap, but the finch has found a remarkable way around its anatomical limitations. The bird simply holds a sharp twig or cactus thorn in its beak and thrusts it into crannies in the bark of a tree, flushing out any insects underneath. When an insect emerges, the finch drops its probe and gobbles the exposed prey. Such employment of tools is rare among birds, but some other songbirds come close to it. The California scrub jay uses the fork of a tree as a vise to hold hard nuts while it hammers them open with its beak. Ravens, like gulls, often fly high in the air with mollusks and crabs and drop them onto rocks to crack the shells, and the European song thrush shucks snails by smashing them against stones.

Displaying the order's adaptive flexibility, some passerines have made their eating habits conform to the ways of man. In Sri Lanka (formerly Ceylon), red-rumped swallows consume large quantities of insects swarming from the grass fires set to clear fields on tea plantations and have learned to hasten to the site at the first sign of smoke. In India, bulbuls make themselves at home in kitchens, where they eat table scraps. Highly urbanized great tits in England have learned how to pry the lids off milk bottles placed on front doorsteps in the morning.

A few seemingly foresighted songbirds store their food. As winter nears, jays and crows often lay in a supply of nuts and grains, supplies that they tuck into the holes and crevices of trees. In northern Europe, their cousins, the nutcrackers, go even further by digging holes and burying collections of hazelnuts in autumn. They have an uncanny ability to locate the nuts months later in the early spring—even when their larders are blanketed under two feet of packed snow. In Australia, the crested bellbird prepares for the dry season by stocking its nest with live grass caterpillars, after squeezing them with its bill to paralyze them. The most bizarre food-storage system, however, is practiced by certain shrikes. Nicknamed butcherbirds, these shrikes prey on small birds, frogs and mammals as well as insects and skewer their victims on thorns and barbed wire for later consumption.

Cedar waxwings eating berries

A Changeable Feast

The thistle is the emblem of Scotland, and it could serve as well for the American goldfinch (right). The handsome little bird is so fond of the prickly purple weed's flowers—a mainstay in its diet—that often as not it will build its nest in a thistle bush. But goldfinches, like the other birds on these pages, are not so finicky that they will not eat other foods. When thistles are out of season, the stout-billed birds subsist on seeds, insects, dandelions and other weeds. The North American Clark's nutcracker (below), a western mountain bird, prefers the nuts of the piñon to all other food, but in winter when there are no piñon nuts, it preys on small mammals or resorts to scavenging, pilfering from campers on the lower slopes. Acorns are the perquisite of the scrub jay (opposite, below). When their usual diet is out of season, many seed- and nut-eating birds will turn to insects, nectar or fruit.

Clark's nutcracker (above), a study in black and white, spends the winter in mountain forests, seldom venturing into the valleys. A subspecies, the alpine nutcracker, has learned to survive the bitter mountain winters without migrating or changing its diet. It squirrels away a supply of nuts and seeds, which it can unerringly locate even under eight inches of snow.

The American goldfinch is a member of the genus Carduelis, from the Latin word for thistle. In winter the male (above) loses his bright plumage and becomes almost as drab as his mate until spring courtship time.

The scrub jay (below) wears the family's characteristic blue feathers but lacks the blue jay's familiar crest. Common in the American West, it lives in chaparral, where its favorite acorns are abundant in the fall.

A dogwood berry is winter provender for a hermit thrush (above), the "American nightingale," which ranges through the continental United States. In summer, insects, spiders and other arthropods fill the hermit's bill of fare.

The skeptical eyes of the yellow-throated miner birds at right belie the relish with which they search for insects. Natives of Australia, miners also subsist on honey, wild fruit and berries.

In menacing dark clouds, red-billed queleas descend like Biblical locust plagues on the grain fields of southern Africa, wiping out entire harvests and often causing disastrous famines. The queleas—sometimes called diochs—are among the most numerous of all birds and one of the world's major crop pests. Extremely gregarious, they flock together in mind-boggling numbers. When they breed they may weave as many as 10 million nests in a single colony, spread out over 500 or more acres of African savanna. Their woven nests are the work of the male birds, which share with their mates the task of rearing the young and remain monogamous through the breeding season. Against the constant threat to

their crops, farmers from Somalia to Senegal and southward to Namibia have struggled for years to destroy the queleas by any means—including poisons, explosives and flamethrowers. But, though some authorities predict that the red-billed birds are doomed to extinction like the passenger pigeon, the queleas show no sign of declining numbers.

Oxpeckers perform two services for their hosts: consuming bloodsucking ticks (above) and raucously warning of the approach of enemies.

The pearly vented tody tyrant (right), a denizen of tropical American woodlands, belongs to the enormous family of tyrant flycatchers. The name is a misnomer, for these birds rarely if ever tyrannize over smaller birds but are known instead for their courageous defense of eggs and nestlings from hawks, snakes and other large predators.

Bug Off

Humanity owes a debt to the small birds shown here, for they are among the world's greatest destroyers of insects and related pests. The yellow-billed oxpecker, an African member of the starling family, lives in symbiotic harmony with large wild animals such as the buffalo at left and domestic cattle, picking off the ticks that infest their bodies. Tody tyrants, members of the largest avian family of the Western Hemisphere—the tyrant flycatchers—subsist on insects and caterpillars (left, below), which they may catch, according to their species, on the wing, from the jungle floor or hopping from leaf to leaf.

While the tyrant flycatchers occupy one of the largest habitats on earth, ranging from Alaska's polar zone to Tierra del Fuego, the woodpecker finch has one of the smallest, confined to only 10 islands in the Galápagos archipelago. Woodpecker finches are among the few animals besides man to use tools, employing a thorn or twig or cactus spine (below) to probe for insects.

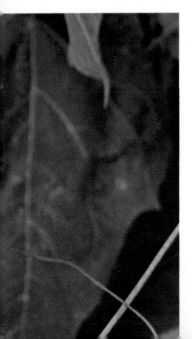

The woodpecker finch (right) occupies an environmental niche in the Galápagos Islands that is filled elsewhere by true woodpeckers. Like its namesake, the tiny finch bores holes in trees for insects with its sharp bill, but, lacking the woodpecker's long, probing tongue, it has ingeniously made use of tools—a twig or spine from a prickly pear cactus—to nudge the grubs or insects out in the open where it can get at them. Only one other bird, the closely related mangrove finch, another Galápagos Islander, has learned to winkle out its food with similar tools.

The handsome male boat-tailed grackle feeding on a dead carp (above) is a noisy habitué of waterfronts from Delaware to Louisiana that gets his name from his keel-shaped tail. His mate, a drab brown and four inches shorter than the 17-inch male, is as dowdy as he is good-looking. Shrikes, one of the few predators among the songbirds, have earned their nickname "butcherbirds" from their habit of impaling their victims on thorns, like the northern shrike with a skewered mouse at right. Shrikes hang up their prey—small birds and mammals, lizards, snakes and large insects—as a means of storage for future meals.

Migration

When Aristotle, one of the keenest observers in the ancient world, awoke one autumn morning to discover that once again the redstarts had vanished as mysteriously as they had come in spring and that they had been replaced by an equal population of robins, he came to this conclusion: The redstarts had been transformed into robins. Actually the redstarts had taken off to winter in Africa while the robins were returning to Greece from their summer homes in northern Europe. For centuries most reasonable men considered Aristotle's explanation perfectly plausible. They knew that some big birds, such as cranes, migrated, but it was inconceivable that tiny songbirds would be capable of undertaking an arduous journey of hundreds or even thousands of miles—unless, as a few surmised, they rode on the backs of the larger migrants. Even as late as the 18th century the great naturalist Linnaeus declared that house martins wintered under the roofs of houses and that their cousins the swallows hibernated in mud.

The misunderstanding surrounding the migration of songbirds may be explained partly by the fact that most travel under the cover of darkness and are rarely seen on their biannual commutation between summer breeding grounds and winter retreats. Many of the nocturnal migrants also journey alone or in small, loose flocks, making it even harder to tell what they are up to. For creatures as small as songbirds, night travel has definite advantages. They are less likely to be spotted by hawks, gulls and other predators. And since small birds burn up their food reserves very quickly, it leaves their days free to refuel. The birds that travel by day tend to be insectivores, such as swallows, which catch their meals on the wing, or else, like starlings, blackbirds and some finches, they mass in large flocks, gaining safety in numbers.

Although most passerines in northerly climates seem to be fair-weather visitors who decamp in the first chill of autumn—and sometimes before—migration is more intimately linked to food than to weather. Most birds adapt well to changes in climate and are capable of withstanding all but the most brutal of winters if they have a ready supply of food. Rather than undertake a long trip to Mexico and Central America with their fellows, some northern orioles, for example, will stay behind, relying on a bird feeder for winter provender in snowy New England. And many songbirds go only as far south as the nearest adequate food supply. The American robin and some blackbirds which probe the ground for food stop in those southern states where the earth remains soft and unfrozen. Most seed-eating birds move just south of the snow belt where grain and nuts remain uncovered. The evening grosbeak that summers in the Upper Peninsula of Michigan migrates due east instead of south, presumably because it can find a better supply of seeds in the more temperate Atlantic Coast states at the same latitude.

In many species, some members migrate and others do not—and again, the availability of food is the main reason. Certain bluebirds, blue jays and magpies that breed in Canada and the northern United States move south in winter where they join their kin who are year-round residents. In Europe, skylarks and wood larks leave Scandinavia for Africa at the end of summer, but the same birds remain in England, where food and winter accommodations are sufficient to stem any wanderlust.

Some songbirds, however, are more adventurous, taking a journey of a couple of thousand rather than a few hundred miles. The great majority of North American passerine migrants retreat with the onset of cold weather into Mexico, Central America and the West Indies, with some going as far as the northern regions of South America. A few even go farther and hold the record among land birds for long-distance travel. The bobolink covers 7,000 miles going from the meadows of Canada to the Argentine pampas. And some swallows travel up to 9,000 miles from Alaska almost to the tip of South America.

Despite the length of their journey, swallows are able to maintain a cruising speed of only about 30 miles an hour—low compared to the 50 miles per hour averaged by ducks and shore birds. But this is much more than that of most other passerines, which put in a grueling six to eight hours a day doing little better than 20 miles an hour. And in attaining even this speed they are usually aided by favorable tailwinds, moving north in spring on a warm air mass and south in fall on an advancing cold front. Still, the tiny songbirds are capable of amazing feats of endurance. Though most migrators must stop to feed, some traverse a 500-mile crossing of the Gulf of Mexico in 16 to 20 hours of continuous, uninterrupted flying. A few cross the inhospitable Sahara without resting for 60 hours. But the record holder for stamina is probably the sedge warbler, which makes a nonstop flight from northern Europe to Africa in four days and nights.

Yellow-headed blackbirds on the move

On the Wing

During their migratory treks, songbirds employ a certain type of aerodynamics—propelled flight, which involves the steady and regular flapping or beating of the wings. The bird must make constant, rapid adjustments in the shape and position of its wings and feathers in order to obtain lift, drive, balance and airborne direction. Except for the yellow-headed blackbird (opposite, top), the birds shown here were photographed under controlled conditions and illustrate various flight postures.

Only the inner half of a bird's wing—the area between its shoulder and wrist—is used for lift, functioning much like the wing of an airplane. The outer half, or tip, with its long primary feathers, acts as a propeller. In flapping flight, the downstroke of the wing propels the bird forward; the upstroke serves only as a stabilizer, maintaining lift. Along with its wing feathers, a bird's tail feathers provide important auxiliary systems of flight. By twisting its tail the bird is able to stop or to steer to either side or up and down. And by fanning out the feathers of its tail the bird acquires an additional lifting or braking surface.

Wings arched, tail outstretched, an American robin heads skyward. Aptly described by its Latin name Turdus migratorius, the robin is a long-distance flier breeding as far north as Canada and Alaska and wintering as far south as Central America.

A cedar waxwing hovers in the air just before landing. Waxwings are irregular migrants that can be found almost everywhere in the United States throughout the year. Those that do journey south usually make the trip only when they are subjected to extreme or unusual cold.

A lesser goldfinch (below) extends its legs and unfurls its wings as it swoops toward a perch. At the onset of autumn most goldfinches leave their breeding grounds and travel in flocks toward Mexico.

The bright yellow crown and white epaulets identify the gliding bird above as a male yellow-headed blackbird. These birds migrate in flocks that are often segregated by sexes, coming together only to breed.

Star Trekkers

Ornithologists have long been intrigued by the questions raised by avian migration, especially those relating to the mysteries of navigation. Each year thousands of birds are caught in mist nets (below) and are either banded and released, to be followed by field investigators who try to determine their migratory patterns, or they are used in various laboratory tests such as those being undertaken by Dr. Stephen T. Emlen of Cornell University in Ithaca, New York.

Dr. Emlen works on the widely accepted premise that migrating birds depend on a variety of cues to determine their flight direction; for night migrants like the indigo bunting, orientation by the patterns of the stars seems to be of major importance. To demonstrate how these cues operate, Dr. Emlen—knowing that caged migratory birds become restless during the months when they would normally migrate—placed indigo buntings in funnel-shaped cages that blocked their view of the horizon, allowing them to see only the stars. The cages' sides were blotting paper folded over an ink-pad base, so that the birds left telltale footprints as they responded to the stars. They were exposed to both the natural night sky and the artificial skies that Emlen created in a planetarium. He proved that autumnal skies made the birds move to the south of their cages, while spring skies resulted in a northward move.

Startled but unharmed, a white-eyed vireo sits trapped in the tangle of a mist net. The bird will be freed after a numbered aluminum band is placed around one of its legs. Sightings of banded birds provide information about migration routes, flight speeds and life-spans that would otherwise be difficult to obtain.

The projector at the Longway Planetarium in Flint, Michigan is silhouetted against an artificially sunlit sky along with seven of Dr. Stephen Emlen's test cages. Inside the cages the buntings were exposed to various projected seasonal star patterns and to a totally starless sky that produced confused activity.

Dr. Stephen Emlen adjusts the cages he designed to monitor the movements of indigo buntings restless to migrate.

117

1,000,000 Birders on the Watch

With a good pair of binoculars as the only essential equipment, birdwatching since World War II has grown into a major spectator sport. One statistician calculates the number of "birders" in the United States at more than one million, not counting other millions of casual backyard watchers. Ornithology is unusual among sciences in that it offers so many opportunities for nonprofessionals to con-

tribute, and indeed, in the years since John James Audubon banded the first bird in North America in 1803, amateurs have taken over a lion's share of the banding of more than a half-million birds annually. Quantities of information have been collected—invaluable for studies of migration and also for determining the life-spans and travel speeds of birds.

Amateurs are of major importance, too, in the annual Christmas census sponsored by the National Audubon Society. Birders, like those above in a Massachusetts meadow, gather in the same areas each year to spot as many birds as possible in a single 24-hour period. The data they collect is crucial in estimating avian populations as well as recording shifts in their composition and relating such shifts to environmental changes.

These Children of the Wind

by Carl Sandburg

In the tradition of the great poet Walt Whitman, Carl Sandburg, born in 1878, celebrated America. His poetry is distinguished by its realism, by the poet's use of man's common speech and slang. In the following excerpt from Sandburg's masterpiece, The People, Yes *(1930), a combination of history, tales and plain gossip, Sandburg records the uncanny return of two purple martins to their home on the shores of Lake Michigan from a Caribbean island where they had been taken and released.*

On the shores of Lake Michigan
high on a wooden pole, in a box,
two purple martins had a home
and taken away down to Martinique
and let loose, they flew home,
thousands of miles to be home again.
   And this has lights of wonder
   echo and pace and echo again.
The birds let out began flying
north north-by-west north

till they were back home.
How their instruments told them
of ceiling, temperature, air pressure,
how their control-boards gave them
reports of fuel, ignition, speeds,
is out of the record, out.
   Across spaces of sun and cloud,
in rain and fog, through air pockets,
wind with them, wind against them,
stopping for subsistence rations,

whirling in gust and spiral,
these people of the air,
these children of the wind,
had a sense of where to go and how,
how to go north north-by-west north,
till they came to one wooden pole,
till they were home again.
    And this has lights of wonder
    echo and pace and echo again
for other children, other people, yes.

A mockingbird's dappled plumage makes it stand out against the red berries of a fire thornbush (above). The master mimics are generally nonmigratory, although birds nesting in the north tend to move south in extreme cold.

Bodies insulated by 3,100 heat-trapping feathers, four house sparrows (left) wait out a winter storm. Eating anything from crumbs to seeds, they have no need to migrate.

A male cardinal (opposite) fluffs out his feathers to ward off the cold. Cardinals are nonmigratory birds whose range has extended because in northern winters they can find food in suburban bird feeders.

The Stay-at-homes

Although the migration of most birds usually coincides with approaching chilly weather, a change of habitat is not merely a means of escaping the bitter cold. It is much more integrally involved with the bird's search for food and with the effect that changes in climate have on an area's food supply. Thus tropical birds tend to migrate during the rainy season, and in the extreme heat of summer desert-dwelling species also relocate. In general, however, it is the winter that takes the greatest toll on a bird's environment: The food supply is diminished, the daylight hours for hunting food are curtailed and the energy needed to keep warm must be increased.

Some birds, including the three pictured on these pages, have overcome these limitations by changing their diets to include food available in winter, by relying on provisions supplied to them by man and by growing more feathers to protect them against the cold. They are able to survive in the areas in which they were raised; at worst they need only to spread out in the general vicinity of their breeding sites without having to migrate to entirely different locales.

A fluttering cloud of tree swallows darkens the autumn sky (above). Tree swallows are among the last of the seven North American swallow species to leave their breeding grounds in the north and the earliest to return in spring. Adaptable birds, they feed on seeds and berries as well as insects.